Voices

VOICES

Edited by

Lydia Cosentino

Dramaline Publications

Dramaline Publications
36-851 Palm View Road
Rancho Mirage, CA 92270
Phone 619/770-6076 Fax 619/770-4507

Library of Congress Cataloging-in-Publication Data

Voices / edited by Lydia Cosentino
        p. cm.
     ISBN O-940669-32-3
     1. Monologues. 2. Acting—Auditions. I. Cosentino, Lydia.
PN2080.V64   1995
808.82'45—dc20   95-45223

This book is printed on 55# Glatfelter acid-free paper, a paper that meets the requirements of the American Standard of Permanence of paper for printed library material.

Contents

INTRODUCTION

The following dramatic monologues were chosen to provide female actors with a rich variety of voices with which to showcase their acting skills. In order to do this, I selected, from 18th- and 19th-century writings, characters of varying ages, from distinct economic backgrounds, in different social positions, and in specific dramatic situations. In the introductions that precede the monologues, I sketched plot and background and described the scene the speakers were in to allow actors to get as much of a feel as possible for the dramatic or comedic intent of the piece.

Some selections are fairly self-explanatory, so I kept their introductions brief. All of the pieces have been timed and have been cut so as not to exceed the three-minute presentation time for an audition—some are much shorter. In some instances, I spliced together speeches, cutting out or around other characters speaking in the scene, creating a female monologue where originally there had been dialogue. I tried, however, to keep the intent of the scene and, where necessary, to describe the other character in the introduction to enable the actor to create the dramatic presence of her listener.

As you read through the scenes, you will hear these women's voices in their diversity and range and be able to choose those for auditions that will show your dramatic and comedic possibilities. I not only selected pieces for the individual variety of the characters but also for the scope of their acting possibilities, so Medea in her tragic rage is balanced against the humorously lustful Lady Booby trying to reason herself out of her passion for her handsome footman.

Since many of these selections are dramatic monologues, you will need to develop a strong image of the other character to whom you are speaking. In the selection from *The Conscious Lovers*, for example, Indiana is speaking to Mr. Sealand, who turns out to be her father, and—in the true fashion of 18th-century comedy—unites her with the lover she thinks she is losing. During the speech, though, you should image this fatherly, compassionate figure who is so sympathetic to you that he is in danger of censuring the blameless Bevil, so even as you dissolve in grief and despair, the lines that deny any blame to Bevil should be spoken passionately and sincerely. Likewise, Millamant's speech from Congreve's *The Way of the World* requires a strong sense of Mirabel's (her lover's) presence in order for her coquettish behavior and playful tone to have substance.

However, you may imagine other selections as soliloquies such as Olivia's in "Some Sharp Truths" and Lady Booby's from Fielding's *Joseph Andrews*. Olivia has returned to a dull and stifling marriage, a marriage she was trapped into because no one told the truth about marriage or women's lives, so she is determined at least to *think* the truth and not lose sight of it. Lady Booby, on the other hand, is torn between her physical passion (which is overpowering and should be physically obvious) and her social snobbery. She is self-deceiving and really looking for a way to rationalize indulging her passion, so she can be played with a broad physical humor. And, then, some characters may speak earnestly to an unknown or unspecified audience, like Elizabeth Cady Stanton does when she recounts the painful experience of being unable to satisfy her father's need for a son in "You Should Have Been a Boy," or the unnamed speakers who describe their lives as needleworkers or barmaids or mothers.

I tried, whenever possible, to give physical descriptions as well as to set the dramatic scenes, but often the speeches themselves will give clues to the type of character who is speaking, and, needless to say, your own creative imaginations are free to create the character physically as well as dramatically, even those from history such as "Mother" Jones—though you'd be hard-pressed to improve on her dramatic presence with her white hair, dusty shoes, old black umbrella, and rather stout build and the striking contrast of her rough speech and high falsetto voice. Similarly, the soft voice and timid presence of the nameless Japanese mother in "The Loss of a Child" helps to stress her grief and loss.

You can choose your costumes with some freedom also. If you want to be historically accurate, the dates are given and some minor research at a local library should yield pictures of dress of the period, and a costume shop or thrift store should produce the items of dress you want. However, since you're striving to create a character, some careful studying of the scene and attention to both the monologue itself and to the information in the introduction should allow you to choose appropriate makeup and costume to enhance the sense of the character you're portraying without requiring you to adhere to historically accurate dressing. After all, Millamant may be an 18th-century seductress, but there's nothing in her speech that dates her ideas. If Medea's language seems too stilted, feel free to smooth it out or update it. For example, she can say (if costuming suggests it), "On me has fallen this. . . ." rather than "On me hath fallen this. . . ." or "as well you know" instead of "as well thou knowst." I think you get the point: adjust the speech to work with your costuming and makeup and intention.

Very few of the monologues require props, though you can use whatever makes the character more real for you and for your audience. For instance, "Mother" Jones benefits from her old, rusty, black umbrella; in "My Past," Miss Julie drinks as she talks; and Lady Etheridege in "A Mother" should have a hand mirror as well as Lady Windermere's fan, which she has come to return. In "The Piece Mistress," the speaker refers to some patched and broken crockery; you may want to cut those early references out if you don't want to use the props. Other less-obvious props may help you develop characterizations—handkerchiefs for twisting, for example, or other objects to concentrate on—let your imagination and the text be your guide.

Although none of the monologues exceed three minutes presentation time, some are a little lengthy, so I have suggested places to cut. In Jane Shore's speech, I suggested two places it could be cut to shorten it; in other monologues, I also suggested places you could cut; however, in other speeches, you may decide to cut parts out for brevity yourself.

Many of these selections could be used also in acting classes to give students chances to create characters and develop scenes through dramatic monologues. The scenes themselves are either explained in the introduction or apparent from the speaker's words. In the cast of characters here assembled, acting students could practice their characterization techniques. There is the invalid, elderly lady in "Sad Memories" who remembers the lover who died in her arms thirty years before, or the rough and hardened Calamity Jane, who yearns to see her daughter, or the woman from "The Most Violent Woman in the Neighborhood" who says, "Passionate! I believe yer. I knocked my father down and well nigh killed him with a flat-iron before I was twelve year old." Then there's the conviction and strength of Antigone, who asks her Uncle, the King, "Wouldst thou do more than slay me? Why, then, dost thou delay?" or the saucy and hard-headed businesswoman, Roxanna, who says, "I supposed when he got to bed with me, he thought himself sure of me; and indeed, in the ordinary course of things, after he had lain with me, he ought to think so," but, of course, with Roxanna, it's not "the ordinary course of things" since she thinks "marriage is a dear way of purchasing [women's] ease; for very often," she continues, "when the trouble was taken off their hands, so was their money, too."

Finally, these scenes provide a historical portrait of women in the 18th and 19th centuries. From both fictional and historical sources, from Greek tragedies and 18th-century dramas, from 18th-century and Victorian novels, from slave narratives and suffragists' speeches, from letters and from diaries, and from the mouths of the poor and downtrodden and the aristocratic and middle-class, we can draw a better picture of who our ancestresses were. As they tell us in their own voices, to be a woman is often to be as different as it is to be the same. In "To Be a Woman," Ruth Benedict, later a well-known anthropologist, felt when she was growing up that "it seems a very terrible thing to be a woman," while Giorgione Willoughby, a fictional character in the 19th-century novel *A Woman of Genius*, glories in her beauty and power as a woman in "Just Before the Wedding": "I am his crown. See me! How singularly, gloriously beautiful!" In "A New Servitude," Jane Eyre, Brontë's fictional governess, yearns for "liberty; for liberty I gasped; for liberty I uttered a prayer . . . I abandoned it and framed a humbler supplication . . . grant me at least a new servitude!" while, in "Human Rights," "Mother" Jones, the 19th-century labor organizer, says, "I have never had the vote, and I have raised hell all over this country! You don't need a vote to raise hell! You need convictions and a voice!" In "A Dangerous Woman," Millwood, an 18th-century seductress in Lillo's *A London Merchant*, claims that her beauty "first made me a wretch, and still continues me so. Men, however generous or sincere to one another, are all self-ish hypocrites in their affairs with us," while Barbara Leigh Smith Bodichon, in "Be Noble, Be Useful, Be Wise," exhorts, "Oh young girls! waiting listlessly for someone to come and marry you; wasting the glorious springtime of your lives sowing nothing but vanity, what a barren autumn will come to you!" Then, however, there's the drawer in "Working in the Mines" who says, "I have a belt 'round my waist, and a chain passing between my legs, and I go on my hands and feet," or the needleworker sewing convict uniforms who tells us, "I works from nine in the morning till eleven at night" and "I haven't no shawl to my back—no, as true as God I haven't." In "The Aftermath," Jane Shore, a hapless mistress of a King, reminds us, "That man, the lawless libertine, may rove free and unquestioned through the wilds of love; while woman, sense and nature's easy fool, if poor, weak woman swerve from virtue's rule, if, strongly charm'd, she leave the thorny way, and in the softer paths of pleasure stray; ruin ensues, reproach and endless shame, and one false step entirely damns her fame." She's echoed by the nameless young woman in "Seduced" who describes her seduction and says, "He left me in the morning, and I have never seen him since. When I returned to my situation, I was discharged immediately." Medea, on the other hand, refuses to remain a victim: "In all else full of fears is woman, a mere coward to face steel in battle, but in the hour she is wronged in wedlock, there is no spirit more murderous than hers"—a fact she goes on to prove by killing her own two beloved children to make their father, Jason, her betrayer, suffer. Or Lysistrata ("she who disbands armies"), who says, "We bear more than twice as much as you [men]. First, we bear children and send off our sons as soldiers. Then, when we ought to be happy and enjoy our youth, we sleep alone because of your expeditions abroad," and she finally forces the men to come home. Or a favorite of mine, Roxanna, who recognizes the dangers of marriage for women when she tells her lover, "It is not you, says I, that I suspect, but the laws of matrimony put the power into your hands; bids you do it; commands you to command; and binds me, forsooth, to obey; you that are now upon even terms with me, and I with you, says I, are the next hour set up upon the throne, and the humble wife placed at your footstool; all the rest, all that you call oneness of interest, mutual affection, and the like, is courtesy and kindness then, and a woman is, indeed, infinitely obliged where she meets with it, but can't help herself where it fails." Roxanna's words, though written in the 18th century by Daniel Defoe, sound pretty similar to Ann Richelieu Lamb's in the 19th-century's "Unequal": "Nothing, however, seems at present to be known than the rule of 'Wives *obey* your husbands!' no matter how silly, how absurd—nay, indeed, in many instances, how ruinous the command may be."

As you can see, whether in fiction or in history, these voices illuminate an aspect of womanhood we recognize even today. We may no longer wear crinolines like the one that went ablaze in "The Perils of the Crinoline" or need to argue that women should be permitted to earn their own livelihood as Lamb does, and it's no longer true that "dey just puts black folks together in the sight of man and not in de sight of God, and dey put dem asunder, too," but the male cadets cheered Sharon Faulkner's defeat, and Clarence Thomas—not Anita Hill—was believed and made a Supreme Court Justice. *Fatal Attraction* was a hit movie, and African-American males protested *The Color Purple*. Fashion and media depict women in short, little-girl dresses or in little-boy short haircuts and hard makeup—the Madonna or the whore dichotomy continues to prevail. Women, however, in Hollywood, are demanding better roles for women over twenty—Ann-Margaret in *Grumpy Old Men* and Susan Sarandon in *Little Women* or Jessica Tandy and Kathy Bates in *Fried Green Tomatoes*—so the sweep of voices in this volume, while originating in 18th- and 19th-century works, resonates for today's actor as well—both in their diversity and in the feelings they express.

GIORGIONE WILLOUGHBY

In The Amber Gods *by Harriet Prescott Spofford (1860), the heroine, Giorgione Willoughby, is an imaginative and sensual young woman whose self-absorption is almost frightening. She says she's "a blonde, none of your silver-washed things—I'm a golden blonde, not too tall—five feet four; not slight, or I couldn't have such perfect roundings." Giorgione's tone of admiration when describing herself is so worshipful that it almost seems she's observing a work of art rather than herself, which may dilute some of the vanity. She has stolen the love of Vaughn Rose, her sister's lover, and is about to marry him. It is a few hours before the wedding when her sister, Lu, the typically self-sacrificing heroine of 19th-century fiction, comes to her and says, "Yone, I want you to tell me if you love him. I love you very much, dear. I only want to know if you will make him happy." She has just assured her sister that she does indeed love him, that "when he forgets me—I shall die!" Her self-absorbed tone becomes almost hypnotic. She looks into a full-length pier mirror as she speaks, and has her bridal veil, perhaps on a stand near her.*

Just Before the Wedding

But I didn't tell Lu quite the truth, you must know. I don't think I should die, except to my former self, if Rose ceased to love me. I should change. Oh, I should hate him! Hate is as intense as love.

Bless me! What time can it be? There are Papa and Rose walking in the garden. I turned out my maid to find chance for all this talk; I must ring for her. There, there's my hair! silken coil after coil, full of broken lights, rippling below the knees, fine and fragrant. Who could have such hair but I? I am the last of the Willoughbys, a decayed race, and from such strong decay what blossom less gorgeous should spring?

October now. All the world swings at the top of its beauty; and those hills where we shall live, what robes of color fold them! Tawny filemont gilding the valleys, each seam and rut a scroll or arabesque, and all the year pouring out her heart's blood to flush the maples, the

great empurpled granites warm with the sunshine they have drunk all
summer! So I am to be married today, at noon I like it best so; it is
my hour. There is my veil, that regal Venice point. Fling it 'round
you. No, you would look like a ghost in one—Lu like a corpse. Dear
me! That's the second time I've rung for Carmine. I dare say the
hussy is trying on my gown. You think it strange I don't delay? Why,
child, why tempt Providence? Once mine, always mine. He might
wake up. No, no, I couldn't have meant that! It is not possible that I
have merely led him into a region of richer dyes, lapped him in this
vision of color, kindled his heart to such a flame, that it may light
him toward further effort. Can you believe that he will slip from me
and return to one in better harmony with him? Is anyone? Will he
ever find himself with that love lost, this love exhausted, only his art
left him? Never! I am his crown. See me! how singularly, gloriously
beautiful! For him only! all for him! I love him! I cannot, I will not
lose him! I defy Fate! Hush—one, two, twelve o'clock. Carmine!

ANN RICHELIEU LAMB

In 1844, Ann Richelieu Lamb said that since women have no power economically, it's ridiculous to claim a spiritual superiority: "Woman," she says, "not being permitted by our current social arrangements and conventional rules to procure a livelihood through her own exertions, is compelled *to unite herself with someone who can provide for her"; therefore, she must attempt to please man, not to uplift him—she becomes what he wants. As you speak the following, you must hear the counter-arguments: "Oh, why are mothers in such haste to delegate to others the delightful task that Providence has assigned to them? They, as the guardian angel of man's infancy, are charged with a mission; to them is committed the implanting of that heavenly germ, to which God must indeed give the increase, but for the early culture of which they are answerable."*

Unequal

Nothing, however, seems at present to be known than the rule of "Wives *obey* your husbands!" no matter how silly, how absurd—nay, indeed, in many instances, how ruinous the command may be. The duty of the wife *means* the obedience of a Turkish slave, while the husband believes himself empowered to be of a like imperviousness with the follower of the turbaned prophet.

It is a curious fact that we never hear the faintest echo of that equally distinct command, "Men, love and *honor* your wives!" It seems to be taken for granted that women have many obligations in this state to perform, from which men are free, but this is far from being the case: the obligations being the same and equally binding upon both, though from the perverse training to which the sexes are subjected, the whole weight is laid upon those who, from the very falsehood of their education, are the least able to bear it. Woman, chained and fettered, is yet expected to work miracles. Man, however, deems himself free to do as he likes, to spend his money and time as he pleases, and to scold his *patient Griselda,* should she dare to remonstrate about extravance, waste, indolence, or idleness.

He business is to love!! an obey!!!, the three articles of woman's creed. She must on no account reason or suppose herself wiser than her protector and legislator, even should he bring her and her children into beggary.

"MOTHER" MARY JONES

"Mother" Mary Jones is a powerful figure in the American labor movement. She was a widow, a schoolteacher, and dressmaker when she became a union organizer around the age of 50. Her compassion for workers in mines and in factories earned her the title "Mother," and her ferocious tenacity when fighting earned her respect. Armed with a long hatpin that she used to secure a large, flat bonnet to her curly white hair, her gray eyes behind their spectacles glittering, she was a force to contend with. In the following speech, spoken in a strong Irish accent and a high falsetto voice, she tells suffragists what she thinks about their battle for the vote for women.

Human Rights

You must stand for free speech in the streets. I have never had a vote, and I have raised hell all over this country! You don't need a vote to raise hell! You need convictions and a voice!

I am not an anti to anything that will bring freedom to my class, but I am going to be honest with you sincere women who are working for votes for women. The women of Colorado have had the vote for two generations and the working men and women are in slavery. The state is in slavery, vassal to the Colorado Iron and Fuel Company and its subsidiary interest.

I do not believe in women's rights nor in men's rights but in human rights. No matter what your fight, don't be ladylike! God Almighty made women, and the Rockefeller gang of thieves made the ladies.

I have just fought through sixteen months of bitter warfare in Colorado. I have been up against armed mercenaries, but this old woman, without a vote, and with nothing but a hatpin, has scared them.

Organized labor should organize its women along industrial lines. Politics is only the servant of industry. The plutocrats have organized their women. They keep them busy with suffrage and prohibition and charity.

ELIZABETH CADY STANTON

Elizabeth Cady Stanton, perhaps more than any other figure, spans the great age of the women's-rights movement of the 19th century. More radical than any of the other leaders of the movement, she called for the vote for women at the first historic convention in Seneca Falls in the summer of 1848. Married to an abolitionist sympathetic to the cause of women, she had seven children; her daughter Harriet became active with her in the suffrage movement; her granddaughter Nora Stanton Barney continued the family tradition of feminism by becoming the first woman in the United States to receive a degree in engineering. The following excerpt is from her autobiography, Eighty Years and More, *which is dedicated to her life-long friend, Susan B. Anthony, "my steadfast friend for half a century," and bears on the title page this quotation: "Social science affirms that women's place in society marks the level of civilization." In the speech that follows, you can see that as a child she had determination and will, but she was already a victim of a society that, like her father, favored sons and men. She did at least as much—if not more—as any other woman to change that system, so perhaps the incident described here was a necessary early stimulus for this formidable woman. Like any anecdote, it needs to be told with a clear purpose in mind.*

You Should Have Been a Boy

When I was eleven years old, my only brother, who had just graduated from Union College, came home to die. A young man of great talent and promise, he was the pride of my father's heart.

I recall going into the large, darkened parlor and finding the casket, mirrors, and pictures all draped in white, and my father seated, pale and immovable. As he took no notice of me, after standing a long while, I climbed upon his knee, when he mechanically put his arm about me, and, with my head resting against his beating heart, we both sat in silence, he thinking of the wreck of all his hopes in the loss of a dear son, and I wondering what could be said or done to fill the void in his breast. At length he heaved a deep sigh and said: "Oh, my daughter, I wish you were a boy!"

Throwing my arms about his neck, I replied: "I will try to be all my brother was."

All that day and far into the night I pondered the problem of boyhood. I thought that the chief thing to be done in order to equal boys was to be learned and courageous. So I decided to study Greek and learn to manage a horse.

I learned to leap a fence and ditch on horseback. I began to study Latin, Greek, and mathematics with a class of boys in the academy, many of whom were much older than I. For three years one boy kept his place at the head of the class, and I always stood next. Two prizes were offered in Greek. I strove for one and took the second. One thought alone filled my mind: "Now," said I, "my father will be satisfied with me."

I rushed breathless into his office, laid the new Greek Testament, which was my prize, on his table and exclaimed: "There, I got it!" He took up the book, asked me some questions about the class, and, evidently pleased, handed it back to me. Then he kissed me on the forehead and exclaimed, with a sigh, "Ah, you should have been a boy!"

JANE EYRE

Jane Eyre, the plain but strong young heroine of the 19th-century novel by that name, has gone to visit her dying aunt, who had made her childhood so painful. Mrs. Reed lays in a big four-poster bed lit by a lamp. Jane expects to see a face that has relented in its bitterness toward her since her aunt sent for her, but instead she notes the well-known face was "stern, relentless as ever—there was that peculiar eye that nothing could melt; and the somewhat raised, imperious, despotic eyebrow." Aunt Reed is cold, unchanged in her antipathy toward Jane. She seems, however, to feel some guilt or unease concerning Jane, which is why she has sent for her. Without acknowledging Jane's presence, she begins to speak in a querulous and irritated tone.

A Deathbed Confession

I have had more trouble with that child than anyone would believe. Such a burden to be left on my hands—and so much annoyance as she caused me, daily and hourly, with her incomprehensible disposition, and her sudden starts of temper, and her continual, unnatural watching of one's movements! I declare she talked to me once like something mad, or like a fiend—no child ever spoke or looked as she did; I was glad to get her away from the house. What did they do with her at Lowood? The fever broke out there, and many of the pupils died. She, however, did not die: but I said she did—I wish she had died!

I had a dislike to her mother always; for she was my husband's only sister, and a great favorite with him: he opposed the family's disowning her when she made her low marriage; and when news came of her death, he wept like a simpleton. He would send for the baby, though I entreated him rather to put it out to nurse and pay for its maintenance. I hated it the first time I set my eyes on it—a sickly, whining, pining thing! It would wail in its cradle all night long—not screaming heartily like any other child, but whimpering and moaning. Reed pitied it, and he used to nurse it and notice it as if it had been his own: more, indeed, than he ever noticed his own at that age. He would try to make my children friendly to the little beggar: the darlings could not bear it, and he was angry with them when they showed their dislikes. In his last illness, he had it brought continually to his bedside; and but an hour before he died, he bound me by vow to keep the creature. I would as soon have been charged with a pauper brat out of a workhouse: but he was weak, naturally weak. John does not at all resemble his father, and I'm glad of it: John is like me and like my brothers—he is quite a Gibson. Oh, I wish he would cease tormenting me with letters for money! I have no more money to give him: we are getting poor. I must send away half the servants and shut up part of the house; or let it off. I can never submit to do that—yet how are we to get on? Two-thirds of my income goes in paying the interest of mortgages. John gambles dreadfully, and always loses—poor boy! He is beset by sharpers: John is sunk and degraded—his look is frightful—I feel ashamed for him when I see him.

MILLWOOD

Millwood, in George Lillo's The London Merchant *(1731), seduces George Barnwell, a young merchant's assistant. Her character is supposed to serve as a warning to young men about the dangers of the city, but, as Millwood tells us, her beauty "first made me a wretch, and still continues me so. Men, however generous or sincere to one another, are all selfish hypocrites in their affairs with us. We are no otherwise esteemed or regarded by them but as we contribute to their satisfaction." So, for the modern listener, she may seem more of a strong-minded woman than an evil temptress. In the following speech, Millwood, a beautiful woman of about twenty-five, who looks, according to her maid, Lucy, "Killingly, Madam! A little more red, and you'll be irresistible," speaks of her intended seduction of George, a handsome youth of eighteen.*

A Dangerous Woman

It's a general maxim among the knowing part of mankind that a woman without virtue, like a man without honor or honesty, is capable of any action, though never so vile; and yet what pains will they not take, what arts not use, to seduce us from our innocence, and make us contemptible and wicked, even in their own opinions! Then is it not just, the villains, to their cost, should find us so? But guilt makes them suspicious and keeps them on their guard; therefore, we can take advantage only of the young and innocent part of the sex, who, having never injured women, apprehend no injury from them.

Such a one, I think, I have found. As I've passed through the city, I have often observed him, receiving and paying considerable sums of money; from thence I conclude he is employed in affairs of consequence.

The stripling is well made and has a good face.

He is about eighteen, innocent and handsome I'll be vastly happy. Why, if I manage well, I may keep him to myself these two or three years. In fact, if I manage well, I shall have done with him much sooner. Having long had a design on him, and meeting him yesterday, I made a full stop, and, gazing wistfully on his face, asked him his name. He blushed, and bowing very low, answered: "George Barnwell." I begged his pardon for the freedom I had taken, and told him that he was the person I had long wished to see, and to whom I had an affair of importance to communicate at a proper time and place. He named a tavern; I talked of honor and reputation, and invited him to my house. He swallowed the bait, promised to come, and this is the time I expect him. Somebody knocks.

Now, after what manner shall I receive him? Let me consider—what manner of person am I to receive? He is young, innocent, and bashful: therefore I must take care not to put him out of countenance at first. But, then, if I have any skill in physiognomy, he is amorous, and, with a little assistance, will soon get the better of his modesty. I'll trust to nature, who does wonders in these matters. If to seem what one is not, in order to be the better liked for what one really is; if to speak one thing, and mean the direct contrary, be art in a woman—I know nothing of nature.

CALAMITY JANE

Calamity Jane was a woman of the Wild West who defied convention all her life. She worked and rode and fought and drank like a man. In her letters to her daughter, whom she had shipped East to be raised by respectable people, however, we see a woman who loves her child and is often concerned with her own lack of respectability. Under the rough exterior, we often glimpse the softer woman who always finds some "damn fool worse off," to whom she gives money. The following monologue retains the rough and energetic tone of her speech while suggesting the softness of the woman raising orphan children and helping those worse off than her. Jane would be dressed in well-worn jeans and dusty boots.

Not Your Typical Mother

I want to corner the Northern Pacific Railroad officials when they come here, and it won't be but a little while before they arrive. I am planning on having a game with them, and then I will be going to old Virginia to be with you a while. I miss my friend Will Lull to stake me. He was always willing to stake me. One night he loaned me a five-spot, and when I saw him the next morning, I had $1000, but it goes, Janey. Easy come, easy go. I always find some poor damn fool worse off than me and help them to a grubstake or buy some God-forsaken family of children clothing and food. I couldn't eat a mouthful if I saw some poor little brat hungry. I always think of you, darling, and away goes my money. Then I start all over again. I don't figure it's any feather in my cap to act the way I do. I sometimes get a little tipsy, Janey, but I don't harm anyone. I have to do something to forget you and your father, but I am not a fancy woman, Janey; if I were, I wouldn't be nursing and scouting and driving stage. That's what Deadwood and Billings call me. To hell with them, too. The pot can't call the kettle black in either town.

You will have to excuse your mother, Janey; she knows she's queer and half-baked. I am going to see you soon now, but I got to get into a poker game and win $20,000 before I can go to you. I am looking after a girl and boy, and I must tell you, Jackie went to Alaska. These two are older. The girl, sixteen; the Indian boy, eighteen. I am going to take them east with me when I go to see you if I win the poker game with the Northern Pacific Railroad. The boy wants to attend a medical school, and the girl wants to be an actress. I will give them both their chance if I win, and I shall win.

ROSE YORKE

In Charlotte Brontë's Shirley, *Rose Yorke, a rather determined young girl, is reading a gothic novel,* The Italian, *and talking to Caroline Helstone about the future. It's quite clear that Rose has definite plans for her future and does not intend to live the typical life of the middle-class female of the period. Young Rose, however, speaks with the confidence of untried youth who has yet to meet any real disappointments, so her sincerity shows through the following speech—but so does her ingenuity.*

The Best-Laid Plans

And in reading it, you feel as if you were far away from England— really in Italy—under another sort of sky, that blue sky of the south that travelers describe.

It makes me long to travel.

I mean to make a way to do so, if one is not made for me. I cannot live always in Briarfield. The whole world is not very large compared with creation: I must see the outside of our own round planet at least.

First this hemisphere where we live; then the other. I am resolved that my life shall be a life: not a black trace like the toad's buried in marble.

Better to try all things and find all empty than to try nothing and leave your life a blank. To do this is to commit the sin of he who buried his talent in a napkin—despicable sluggard!

If my master has given me ten talents, my duty is to trade with them, and make them ten talents more. Not in the dust of household drawers shall the coin be interred. I will *not* deposit it in a broken-spouted teapot, and shut it up in a china closet among tea things. I will *not* commit it to your worktable to be smothered in piles of woolen hose. I will *not* prison it in the linen press to find shrouds among the sheets: and least of all, mother—least of all will I hide it in a tureen of cold potatoes, to be ranged with bread, butter, pastry, and ham on the shelves of the larder.

The Lord, who gave each of us our talents, will come home someday and will demand from all an account. The teapot, the old stoking foot, the linen rag, the willow-pattern tureen, will yield up their barren deposit in many a house: suffer your daughters, at least, to put their money to the exchangers, that they may be enabled at the Master's coming to pay him his own with usury.

VIOLET

Violet is a 103-year-old African-American who describes how she was persuaded to marry her second husband while she was a slave. Planters encouraged their slaves to marry so they would have children and also so they would be more settled down, but, as Violet tells us, husbands or wives could be sold apart from each other since the marriage did not exist legally: "Dey just puts black folks together in de sight of man and not in de sight of God, and dey put dem asunder, too."

A Slave Marriage

My first husband—nice man; den he sold off to Florida—neber hear from him 'gain. Den I sold up here. Massa want me to breed, so he say, "Violet, you must take some slave here."

Den I say, "No, Massa, I can't take any here." Well den, Missis, he go down Virginia, and he bring up two slaves—and Missis say, "One ob dem's for you, Violet," but I say, "No, Missis, I can't take one ob dem, 'cause I don't lub 'em." By and by, Massa he buy tree more, and den Missis say, "Now, Violet, ones dem is for you." I say, "I do' know—maybe I can't lub one dem neider," but she say, "You must hab one ob dese." Well, so Sam and I, we lib along two year— he watchin' my ways and I watchin' his ways. At last, one night, we was standin' by de woodpile togeder, and de moon bery shine, and I do' know how 'twas, he answer me, he want a wife, but he didn't know where he get one. I say, "Plenty girls in Georgia." He say, "Yes, but maybe I shan't find any I like so well as you." Den I say maybe he wouldn't like my ways, 'cause I'se an ole woman, and I hab four children, and anybody marry me must be jest kind to dem children as dey was to me, else I couldn't lub him. Well, so we went on from one ting to another, till at last we say we'd take one anoder, and so we've libbed togeder eber since.

We just takes one another—we asks de white folks' leave, and den takes one anoder. Some folks, dey's married by de book; but den what's de use? Dere's my fus husband, we'se married by de book, what's de use? Dere's my fus husband, we'se married by de book, and he sold way off to Florida, and I's here.

Dey do what dey please wid us, so we jest make money for dem—and I's had four children by him—and he never slip away from me, nor I from him.

TEMPIE

Tempie describes her marriage to Exter and the custom of jumping over a broom. Slave weddings ranged from a blanket marriage ("he bring his blanket and lay it down beside mine") to a full-scale ceremony with white dress and bridesmaids and minister, but there was never a license nor certificate since the marse (master) could terminate the marriage at will. Because there was no prescribed civil or religious ceremony, slaves devised rituals of their own. The commonest of these was "jumping the broomstick" when the couple would seal their vows by jumping or stepping over a broomstick. Sometimes, however, white masters (marses) would add their own "humorous" touches, such as Tempie describes here.

Tempie's Wedding

Uncle Edmond Kirby married us. He was de slave preacher dat preached at de plantation church. After Uncle Edmond said de last words over me and Exter, Marse George got to have his little fun. He say, "Come on, Exter, you and Tempie got to jump over de broomstick backwards to see which one gwine be boss of your household." Marse George hold de broom about a foot high off de floor. De one dat jump over it backwards, and never touch handle, gwine boss de house. If both of dem jump over without touchin' it, dey won't gwine be no bossin', dey just gwine be congenial.

I jumped first, and I sailed right over dat broomstick same as a cricket. But when Exter jump, he done had a big dram and his feets was so big and clumsy dat dey got all tangled up and fell headlong. Marse George, he laugh and told Exter he gwine be bossed 'twell he scared to speak.

After de weddin' we went down to de cabin Mis' Betty done all dressed up, but Exter couldn't stay no longer den dat night 'cause he belonged to Marse Snipes Durham and he had to go back home.

I was glad when de War stopped 'cause den me and Exter could be together all de time. After we was free, we rented land, den after while we bought a farm. We paid three hundred dollars we done saved. We had a hoss, a steer, a cow, and two pigs besides some chickens and four geese. Den we hitched up de wagon and throwed in de passel of chillen and moved to our new farm.

19-CENTURY JAPANESE WOMAN

In the 19th century, life was hard for Japanese women—marriages were arranged, and there was no economic or social position for single women. If, however, a woman married a poor man, she would have to cook outside in freezing weather and live in a tiny house with only a few mats. Japanese women were humble and submissive, grateful for every small kindness with a childlike piety and self-effacement that was often idealized by Western men, such as Puccini in his opera Madam Butterfly *or the more current* Miss Saigon *(by two French males). In both stories, it is the Asian woman's complete selflessness that appeals to the writers and the viewers. The following excerpt from the diary of a 19th-century Japanese woman who gratefully married a poor man when she was already twenty-nine years old (a very late age to be unmarried) and won his affection "by faultless performance of duty and docility": "Now as I had been carefully watching my husband's ways from the beginning, I knew that he was a very strict man, and I resolved so to conduct myself in all matters as never to cross his will." She is at the other extreme of character from our first entry, Giorgione Willoughby. She bears three children, all of whom die shortly after birth. The following monologue describes the birth, celebration, and death of her third child; the mother dies two weeks later herself. Her grief is expressed in a self-effacing, simple, quiet tone. She will be dressed in traditional Japanese dress. You might cut the last two paragraphs if you want to shorten the piece.*

The Loss of a Child

On the twentieth day of the second month, at six o'clock in the morning, my third child—a boy—was born.

We had expected a girl, but it was a boy who was born, so, when my husband came back from his work, he was greatly surprised and pleased to find that he had a boy.

But the child was not well able to take the breast, so we had to nourish him by means of a feeding bottle.

On the seventh day after the boy's birth, we partly shaved his head. And in the evening we had the seventh-day festival—all by ourselves.

My husband had caught a bad cold sometime before, and he could not go to work next morning, as he was coughing badly. So he remained in the house.

Early in the morning, the child had taken his milk as usual. But, about ten o'clock in the forenoon, he seemed to be suffering great pain in his breast, and he began to moan so strangely that we sent a man for a doctor. Unfortunately, the doctor that we asked to come was out of town, and we were told that he would not come back before night. Therefore, we thought that it would be better to send at once for another doctor, and we sent for one. He said that he would come in the evening. But, about two o'clock in the afternoon, the child's sickness suddenly became worse, and a little before three o'-clock—the twenty-seventh day of the second month (piteous to say!)—my child was dead, having lived for only eight days.

I thought to myself that, even if this new misfortune did not cause my husband to feel an aversion for me, thus having to part with all my children, one after another, must be the punishment of some wrong done in the time of a former life. And, so thinking, I knew that my sleeves would never become dry—that the rain of tears would never cease—that never again in this world would the sky grow clear for me.

And more and more I wondered whether my husband's feelings would not change for the worse, by reason of his having to meet such trouble, over and over again on my account. I felt anxious about his heart, because of what already was in my own.

Nevertheless, he only repeated these words: "From the decrees of Heaven there is no escape."

MARY FAIRFAX SOMERVILLE

Mary Fairfax Somerville grew up in Scotland in the late-18th century, when it was almost impossible for a girl to receive an academic education—much less to study math. In her account of her life, she describes her natural curiosity about science and math and the difficulty she faced trying to learn more about these subjects: "Unfortunately, not one of our acquaintances or relations knew anything of science or natural history; nor, had they done so, should I have had courage to ask them a question, for I should have been laughed at. I was often very sad and forlorn; not a hand held out to help me." With much difficulty, however, she continues to read and educate herself by reading Euclid after household chores are done until her marriage. Then it is not until after her husband's death that she is able to resume her studies. She is middle-aged, practical-looking, and speaks with a Scottish accent.

Getting an Education

I was very much out of health after my first husband's death and chiefly occupied with my children, especially with the one I was nursing; but as I did not go into society, I rose early, and, having plenty of time, I resumed my mathematical studies. I became acquainted with Mr. Wallace, editor of a mathematical journal. I had solved some of the problems contained in it and sent them to him, which led to a correspondence, as Mr. Wallace sent me his own solutions in return. Mine were sometimes right and sometimes wrong, and it occasionally happened that we solved the same problem by different methods. At last I succeeded in solving a prize problem! I was awarded a silver medal cast on purpose with my name, which pleased me exceedingly.

Mr. Wallace was selected Professor of Mathematics in the University of Edinburgh, and was very kind to me. When I told him that I earnestly desired to go through a regular course of mathematical and astronomical science, even including the highest branches, he gave me a list of the requisite books. I was thirty-three years of age when I bought this excellent little library. I could hardly believe that I possessed such a treasure when I looked back on the day that I first saw the mysterious word "algebra," and the long course of years in which I had persevered almost without hope. It taught me never to despair. I had now the means and pursued my studies with increased assiduity; concealment was no longer possible, nor was it attempted. I was considered eccentric and foolish, and my conduct was highly disapproved of by many, especially by some members of my own family. They expected me to entertain and keep a gay house for them, and in that they were disappointed.

CHARLOTTE CARMICHAEL STOPES

Many women had to learn how to speak out in public since their training taught them that it was unladylike to speak out publicly. In fact, the accusation of "strong-mindedness" was the most effective social weapon used against women seeking to be educated or intellectually assertive. Debating and discussion societies were begun in order to give women an opportunity to practice speaking up, but even in these rather protected and supportive environments, women often had difficulty in speaking out, as Charlotte Carmichael Stopes' account reveals. Stopes later went on to become a noted writer on Shakespeare, and her daughter, Marie Stopes, became a well-known advocate for birth control and a sex reformer. She is soft-spoken and somewhat timid (but determined), wears spectacles, and is plain-looking.

My First Speech

For years, I had heard of discussion societies of brothers and male friends, of students in that much-hungered-for University, under whose portals no women could enter as undergraduates. When I was ready for it, I was, however, taken to a real Literary Society. The Misses Mair had formed one among their class fellows and friends in Abercromby Place, Edinburgh, the house of their mother, and a friend introduced me as a member. This was different from other societies of the kind, in having, as the fundamental reason for its existence to include debates, and the very day I joined, the members *discussed* a *Discussion*. We were invited to give our opinion if such an exercise would be desirable. I remember replying: "Yes, I think the discussion the most important part of any society. We can write in any magazine, but we can only learn to speak among ourselves." That was early in 1866.

At the next meeting, we had a debate on the subject "Ought women to be strong-minded?" There was a paper on each side, well-written, timidly read, duly supported, but discussion flagged. It was evidently handicapped by some strong things said against "unwomanly strong-minded women." Suddenly I heard my name called, with a mild reproach that I had not seemed very ready to take the opportunity of learning to speak. I had taught myself that when anything unpleasant had to be done, it was better to get it over than to think about it. So I rose at once. If I relate what followed, it is only for the benefit of beginners. A tearing traffic seemed to have started through the quiet street, salvoes of artillery resounded from the castle, and an earthquake shook the foundations of the rock-built house in which we met. My own sensations matched my surroundings, my ears rang, my head swam, my knees trembled, my back ached, my heart stood still and then tried to beat down its bounds, and a lump stuck in my throat larger than ever Adam's apple grew. I spasmodically gasped, "Ought women to be *weak-minded?*" and then my parched tongue absolutely refused to move further, all the ideas that had been coursing through my brain five minutes before had vanished, and I sat down in shame and confusion. It took half an hour before the storm and tremor ceased, and my heart beat normally.

BARBARA LEIGH SMITH BODICHON

Barbara Leigh Smith Bodichon says, "To think a woman is more feminine because she is frivolous, ignorant, weak, and sickly is absurd; the larger-natured a woman is, the more decidedly feminine she will be; the stronger she is, the more strongly feminine. You do not call a lioness unfeminine, though she is different in size and strength from the domestic cat or mouse." She wants women to work and feel pride in working, to be self-sufficient and proud of that self-sufficiency. Her inspirational energy can be heard in the following passage from an 1856 speech. She would dress in rather severe, dark clothes, wear glasses and, perhaps, a practical hat, and have a strong speaking voice.

Be Noble, Be Useful, Be Wise

Cries are heard on every hand that women are conspiring, that women are discontented, that women are idle, that women are overworked, and that women are out of their sphere. God only knows what is the sphere of any human being.

One great corresponding cry rises from a suffering multitude of women saying, "We want work."

God sent all human beings into the world for the purpose of forwarding, to the utmost of their power, the progress of the world. We must each leave the world a little better than we found it.

No human being has the right to be idle. Whatever land comes under our hands, we should drain and make more fertile forever. The children who are in our power should be educated. If an old pot comes to us to mend, we must mend it as best we can. *And we must train ourselves to do our work well.* Women must, as children of God, be trained to do some work in the world. Women may not take a man as a god: they must not hold their first duty to be toward any human being.

There is nothing in the world so sad, so pitiful to see, as a young woman—who has been handsome, full of youthful joy, animal spirits, and good nature—fading at thirty or thirty-five. Becoming old too soon, getting meager, dried up, sallow, pettish, peevish, the one possible; does it with men? But we ardently desire that women should not make *love their profession.*

Love is not the end of life. It is nothing to be sought for; it should come. If we work, love may meet us in life; if not, we have something still, beyond all price.

Oh young girls! waiting listlessly for someone to come and marry you; wasting the glorious springtime of your lives sowing nothing but vanity, what a barren autumn will come to you! You are trying hard to make yourselves agreeable and attractive by dress and frivolity, and all this time your noblest parts lie sleeping. Arouse yourselves! Awake! Be the best that God has made you. Do not be contented to be charming and fascinating; be noble, be useful, be wise.

ELDERLY WOMAN

In 1849, this elderly woman makes convict uniforms, one of the worst paying of needlework jobs. She lives in a small backroom on the first floor of an old building. She is a thin and aged woman who speaks nervously and stammers. She has been worn down by hard work and poverty, but her clothing is neatly mended.

Convict Labor

I work at convict work, "the grays"; some are half yellow and half brown, but they're all paid the same price. I makes the whole suit. I gets 7 3/4 quid for all of it, jacket, trousers, and waistcoat, and provide my own thread out of that. There's full a day and a half's work in a suit. I works from nine in the morning till eleven at night. In a day and a half, deducting the cost of thread and candles for the suit (to say nothing of firing), I earns 3 3/4 quid—not two quid a day. The other day I had to sell a cup and saucer for a halfpenny, 'cause crockeryware's so cheap—there was no handle to it, it's true—in order to get me a candle to work with.

I can't tell what I average, for sometimes I have work and sometimes I ain't. I could earn three shilling a week if I had as much as I could do, but I don't have it very often. I'm very often very idle. I can assure you I've been trotting about today to see after a shilling job and couldn't get it. There's someone at the door. What a bother there is if a person owes a few halfpence. That's what made me keep the door locked. I suppose her mother has sent for the old shawl she lent me. I haven't no shawl to my back—no, as true as God I haven't; I haven't indeed!

THE PIECE-MISTRESS

A piece-mistress is a person who assigns work (by the piece) to other workers and collects a percentage of the pay. The position is usually thought of as a step up the economic ladder, but as the following account suggests, it is still far from a financially stable position. The woman who speaks is a widow of about fifty who looks older. She is dressed poorly but neatly and speaks with a lower-class London or, perhaps, a New York accent (in which case you can change shillings and quids to dollars). She could sit in front of her battered heater with a scratched pot on a hotplate nearby.

Starved Entirely

Poor people you know is glad to get anything.

Ah, sir, you needn't look at my crockeryware—I'll show it to you. There isn't a whole vessel in the place; only nobody would know but they were sound, you see, to look at 'em. I'm a piece-mistress. I get the work out of warehouse, and give it to the workpeople. I has a penny a pair out of them. I has two pence out of some—they are the sergeants' uniforms. Perhaps I'd get forty pair out in a week, perhaps thirty pair, and maybe ten—when they has them I get them. Before my husband died, I've had 100 pair out in a week.

At the time my husband lived, we did pretty well. Was never out of work. If we hadn't it from one warehouse, we had it from the others we worked for. He has been three years buried next Easter Sunday, and there's many a night since I've went to bed without my supper, myself and my children. Since then I've had nothing, only just a few odd trousers now and then. I had to go to the workhouse last winter, myself and my children; I couldn't get a meal of victuals for them, and this winter I suppose I shall have to go into it again. If I haven't work, I can't pay my rent. Three weeks ago I had only twenty pair to make, and that's one shilling, eight quid for myself and boy to live upon (my other's out in the Marine School), and my rent out of that is one shilling, six quid. My boy gets one shilling, six quid a week besides this, and only for that I couldn't live at all. And that's drawed before it's earned. I'm obliged to have it to pay. I call it a good week if I get forty pair of trousers to give out. This is three shilling, four quid to me, and upon that me and my boy must both live; and there was my other boy to do the same, too, when I had him. I occasionally get a bit of broken victuals from those who know me round about. I little thought I should be so miserable as I am. That fender is not mine. I borrowed it off my landlady; not that saucepan, neither; I got it to boil my potatoes in. Indeed, you may say I very often want. We should be starved entirely if it was not for my landlady, and that's the blessed truth.

THE GENTLEWOMAN

Gentlewomen, that is women from the middle-class, were often thrown into poverty by the death of a husband. This woman, about forty years old but looking much older, lives in someone else's empty house and tries to reconcile her genteel past with her present poverty. She wears a black dress that is tidy, well-worn yet respectable, and has a sewing basket with some children's caps in it. She's soft-spoken and may verge on weak tears during the monologue.

Changed Circumstances (1849)

I work at needlework generally—I profess to do that, indeed, that is what I have done ever since I have been a widow. But it is shocking payment. What I am engaged upon now is from a private lady. I haven't, as yet, made any charge. I don't know what the price will be; I did intend to ask three quid each. The lady has been a great friend to me. They are plain nightcaps that I am making, and are for a lady of rank. Such persons generally, I think, give the least trouble for their work. I can't say how long they take me each to make. I've been very ill, and I've had the children to help me.

The lady won't put the price herself upon the nightcaps, and I feel timid in asking a price of a lady that's been a friend to me. Latterly I've had no work at all, only that which I got from an institution for distressed needlewomen. They were children's chemises. I did the seven chemises in a fortnight, and got seven shillings for them. I have also made white corded-muslin cut across, and the very largest. I have six quid a dozen for hemming them, and had to find the cotton of course. I have often said I would never do any more of them; I thought they would never have been done, there was so much work in them. Myself and daughter hemmed the dozen in a day. It was a day's very hard work. It was really such hard work that I cried over it. I was so ill, and we were wanting food so badly.

That is all myself and daughter have done for this last month. During that time, the two of us (my daughter is eighteen) have earned nine shilling, six quid for four weeks, or two shilling 4 1/2 quid per week. My daughter and I have earned at plain needlework a good deal more than that. But to get more, we have scarcely time to eat. I have, with my daughter's labor and my own, earned as much as ten shilling; but then such hard work injures the health. I should say an industrious quick hand might earn at plain needlework, taking one thing with another, three shillings, six quid a week, if she were fully employed. But there is a great difficulty in getting work—oh, yes, very great. The schools injure the trade greatly. Ladies give their work to the National Schools, and thus needle-women who have families to support are left without employment.

THE BARMAID

Barmaids worked long hours in confining circumstances. In 1913, their hours were finally reduced to sixty-three a week. These young women often looked old before they were out of their teens. She would have a rather slovenly appearance and speak in an uneducated accent.

Inhaling Foul Breath (1876)

Being a barmaid myself for nearly seven years, I speak from experience; and what I say I affirm to be the truth. I live in a city house with six others, and we all work very hard, our hours being seventeen in a day. We open at five-thirty a.m. and close at midnight. Two of us take it in turns to get up a week half past five o'clock and retire at ten o'clock p.m. The rest of us get up at eight o'clock a.m. and are up till we close. We are supposed to have two hours rest each day, but this week we only get three days out of six, and the other three days we have but an hour. We are supposed to be allowed to go out every third Sunday. Several of us have asked to be allowed to go out in rest time to get a breath of fresh air, but we have been refused for fear we should exceed our time. Therefore, from week's end to week's end, we have to inhale smoke, gas, and the foul breath of the people crowding at our bar, and we have no comfort, release, or relaxation from this dreary, wearing toil. I assure you we all feel fit to drop with fatigue, long before the period comes for our short rest.

SARAH ANN ROBERTS

Sarah Ann Roberts, a young woman who is in constant pain and looks in broken health though she is not yet twenty years old, describes working in the field as a child of eleven. Children were often used for field labor because they were small enough to get in places adults could not. The abuse they suffered, however, is well documented: "One [a gangmaster] has used them [the children] most horrible, kicking them, hitting them with fork handles, hurdlesticks, etc., and even knocking them down. It is if the children play or don't mind their work or are a little troublesome," says one mother who was forced to send some of her children to work when they turned age seven after she was left a widow with eleven children. Sarah would be dressed in country clothes, wear big, dirty boots, and be bent over with arthritic pain.

Working on a Field Gang (1867)

Soon after I went out with the gang, when I was eleven perhaps, I got the rheumatism. The work was so wet; we have been dripping through, especially in wheat. When low, it would be up to our knees, and sometimes it was up to our shoulders; we have weeded it when in the ear. I have been so wet that I have taken off my clothes and wrung them out and hung them up to dry on the top of the wheat or anywhere while we went in again to weed. We hang up only light things, such as aprons, and handkerchiefs—not petticoats. We have had to take off our shoes and pour the water out, and then the man would say, "Now then, to it again." Often when it came on to rain, there was no shelter within reach, but, if there was any, sometimes he would not let us go to it till we were drenched. I often blamed him for making my bones sore. The man knocked us about and ill-used us dreadfully with hoes, spuds, and everything—he would not care what. We dared not complain. One ought not to be glad to hear of anyone's death, but a good many children were glad when he died.

BETTY HARRIS

Women often were put to work in the mines by fathers or husbands. There are illustrations of half-naked women harnessed like horses to mining equipment. Their pay was about two shillings a day or less (men earned three shillings, six quid), but for women who lived in otherwise unindustrialized areas, mine work was the only source of wages. Betty Harris, in her late thirties, hardened by labor, dressed neatly but poorly, and speaks in a strong country accent as she describes her work in the mines.

Working in a Mine (1842)

I am a drawer and work from six o'clock in the morning to six at night. Stop about an hour at noon to eat my dinner; have bread and butter for dinner: I get no drink. I have two children, but they are too young to work. I have a belt 'round my waist, and a chain passing between my legs, and I go on my hands and feet. The road is very steep, and we have to hold by a rope; and when there is no rope, by anything we can catch hold of. There are six women and about six boys and girls in the pit I work in: it is very hard work for a woman. The pit is very wet where I work, and the water comes over our clog-tops always, and I have seen it up to my thighs: it rains in at the roof terribly: my clothes are wet through almost all day long. I have drawn till I have had the skin off me: the belt and chain is worse when we are in the family way. My husband has beaten me many a time for not being ready. I were not used to it at first, and he had little patience; I have known many a man beat his drawer. I have known men take liberties with the drawers, and some of the women have bastards.

I think it would be better if we were paid once a week, instead of once a month, for then I could buy my victuals with ready money.

THE SLAVE WOMAN

A sizable number of "fighting, mule-headed" slave women refused to "take foolishness" from anybody. "Fight, and if you can't fight, kick; if you can't kick, then bite," one slave advised her daughter. The following account suggests the speaker is just such a "fighting, mule-headed" woman. She's a large, massive woman with a deep and commanding voice.

Fighting Back

My mother's boss went off deer hunting. While he was gone, the overseer tried to whip her. She knocked him down and tore his face up so that the doctor had to tend to him. When Pennington came back, the overseer told him that he went down to the field to whip the hands and that he just thought he would hit Lucy a few licks, but she jumped on him and like to tore him up. Old Pennington said to him, "Well, if that is the best you could do with her, damned if you won't just have to take it." She could do more work than any two men. There wasn't no use for no one man to try to do nothing with her. No overseer never downed her.

The white folks said I was the meanest slave that ever wuz. One day, my Mistress Lydia called for me to come in the house, but no, I wouldn't go. She walks out and says she is gwine make me go. So she takes and drags me in the house. Then I grabs that white woman and shook her until she begged for mercy. When the master comes in, I wuz given a terrible beating, but I didn't care for I give the mistress a good un, too. Mistress set me to scrubbing up the barroom. I felt a little grum, and didn't do it to suit her; she scolded me about it, and I sassed her; she struck me with her hand. Thinks I, it's a good time now to dress you out, and damned if I won't do it. I set down my tools and squared for a fight. The first whack, I struck her a hell of a blow with my fist. I didn't knock her entirely through the panels of the door, but her landing against the door made a terrible smash, and I hurt her so badly that all were frightened out of their wits and I didn't know myself but what I'd killed the old devil.

LOUISA PICQUET

Louisa Picquet, a Georgia slave, describes her attempted rape by her master when she was fourteen. She was working for Mrs. Bachelor, who owned the boarding house where Cook, her master, stayed when the incident she describes occurred. She's in her twenties, very attractive, and clear-speaking.

Out of the Frying Pan

I was a little girl, not fourteen years old. One day, Mr. Cook told me I must come to his room that night and take care of him. He said he was sick. I told Mrs. Bachelor what Mr. Cook said. Then she whispered with her sister and told me I need not go. At breakfast time I had to take his breakfast up to his room, on a waiter. He had not got up yet. Then he order me to shut the door. At the same time, he was kind of raisin' up out of bed. Before I had time to shut the door, a gentleman walks out of another room close by. Then Mr. Cook said, "What you stand there for, you damn fool? Go 'long downstairs and get me some more salt." Mrs. Bachelor caught my look and said, "Louisa, one of the boys will take that salt up; I want you for a minute." He call out of the window for me to bring him up a pitcher of water. Then he told me I must come to his room that night; if I didn't, he'd give me hell in the mornin'. I promised him I would, for I was afraid to say anything else. Then I came to the conclusion that he could not do anything but whip me, so I didn't go.
In the mornin' he want to know why I didn't come up, and I told him I forget. So he whip me, so that I won't forget another time. I told Mrs. Bachelor that I guess I'd have to go upstairs that night; and ask her what I should do. She said the best plan would be to keep out of his way.
Well, about tea-time, he wanted water. That was sent up. Then he wanted a button sewed on his wristband. Mrs. Bachelor sent him word to send the shirt down and her sister would put a button on for him. Then he sent word that I must come up and get his boots and

black them. About bedtime, he call one of the boys to know if they told me about the boots; and they said they hadn't seen me.

In the mornin', he came to the ironin' room, downstairs, where I was, and whip me with cowhide, naked, so I s'pect I'll take some of the marks with me to the grave.

When he was whippin' me so awfully, I made up my mind 'twas of no use, and I'd go and not be whipped any more. That very day, we was taken by the sheriff and was sold the next mornin'. I tell you, I was glad when I was taken off to be sold, but I jump out of the fryin' pan into the fire.

RUTH BENEDICT

Ruth Benedict, who was a noted anthropologist and a friend of Margaret Meade's, began her life as Ruth Fulton. From the beginning, she was restless and dissatisfied with the lot of being female. As a child, she had tantrums, "outside invasions," which, once cured, were succeeded by depressions. In the following passage, Ruth, aged twenty-five, contemplates being a woman. She is dark and intense and speaks passionately.

To Be a Woman (1912)

I've just come through a year in which I have not dared to think; I seemed to keep my grip only by setting my teeth and playing up to the mask I had chosen. I have not dared to be honest, not even with myself. I could only try to live through day after day, day after day, and not dishonor them overmuch. In spite of myself, bitterness at having lived at all obsessed me; it seemed cruel that I had been born, cruel that, as my family taught me, I must go on living *forever*. Life was a labyrinth of petty turns, and there was no Ariadne who held the clue.

I tried, oh very hard, to believe that our own characters are the justification of it all. But the boredom had gone too deep; I had no flicker of interest in my character. What was my character, anyway? My real *me* was a creature I dared not look upon—it was terrorized by loneliness, frozen by a sense of futility, obsessed by a longing to *stop*. No one had ever heard of that Me. If they had, they would have thought it an interesting pose. The mask was tightly adjusted.

So much of the trouble is because I am a woman. To me it seems a very terrible thing to be a woman. There is one crown that perhaps is worth it all—a great love, a quiet home, and children. We all know that is all that is worthwhile, and yet we must peg away, showing off our wares on the market if we have money, or manufacturing careers for ourselves if we haven't. We have not the motive to prepare ourselves for a "life-work" of teaching, of social work—we know that we would lay it down with hallelujah in the height of our success, to make a home for the right man.

And all the time in the background of our consciousness rings the warning that perhaps the right man will never come. A great love is given to very few. Perhaps this makeshift time-filler of a job *is* our life work after all.

It is all so cruelly wasteful. There are so few ways in which we can compete with men—surely not in teaching or in social work. If we are not to have the chance to fulfill our one potentiality—the power of loving—why were we not born men? At least we could have had an occupation then.

GERTRUDE

Gertrude is the daughter of Polish-Jewish parents brought up in the Midwest in the early 19th century. "I was never," she says, "a leading feminist. I managed time to live, to be a wife, a mother, and to be in charge of my home. I did my daily job also. Was it hard? Of course it was. Did it destroy my strength? Of course it did not." In this reminiscence, Gertrude shows how strong home training can be; when it comes right down to it, Gertrude cannot do what she has been taught not to do. Gertrude is in her late twenties and conservatively dressed.

The Dance

It was perhaps due to my going to high school, mother said, gently and dubiously, that I wanted something new. I wanted to dance, to play, to have fun just like other girls in my classes. I didn't mean to go to work at fourteen or fifteen, marry at sixteen, be a mother at eighteen, and an old woman at thirty. I wanted a new thing—happiness. I was different from my sisters, who thought of marrying as soon as possible.

My mother drew her fine dark brows together. She took my face in her little hands, round and soft, in spite of her constant work. "You shall learn to dance," she said, "my daughter!"

And dance I did. I learned to dance in what, I suppose, was a dreadful public dance hall, for I paid a quarter a lesson there, once every Wednesday night, and I danced with the lady instructor when she thought of me; but I faithfully put my foot out—one, two, three, and turn—as the long line of men and women learned the steps of the waltz. I learned to two-step, and to schottische, and even—wild days, those—to do the barn dance. Mother took me to the hall and came to take me back home at eleven.

Then I went to a dance. I went with Jack, a blue-eyed boy from my class, and wore a dress of mother's cut down and made to fit me. I did not tell her I was going with a Gentile. I simply told her I was going to a dance at school.

My swain met me after school, and we walked up together to the chapel, there to talk until the pianist arrived, for we had no brass bands then. The room became crowded. He put out his arms and said, "Shall we dance?"

Before me came my father's face, still and austere. I felt something chill me.

"Oh, Jack," I said. "I—I don't feel well. I'm going home."

And home I went. I could not dance with a Gentile.

MARY ANN

Many young girls were seduced and led into a life of prostitution in the 19th century. An attempt was often made to rescue these "fallen" women, and accounts such as the following were made public to warn "respectable" girls. Mary Ann, the girl who speaks, is dressed neatly but cheaply and, perhaps, a bit gaudily.

Seduced (1860)

I am twenty years of age. My mother was a pious woman who sent me, and my brothers and sisters, to a Sunday School. I was brought up to London by an uncle who kept a public-house. After teaching me the business, he procured for me a situation as a barmaid. One evening, as I was going to my uncle's house, I was accosted by a gentleman, who asked me to take a walk with him, and proposed that we should go to Astley's Theatre. To this I at first objected. However, upon his promising that I should leave the theatre early, I was induced to go there with him. The time passed away so rapidly, that when we came out, it was much past the hour I ought to have been at home, which threw me into great distress of mind; and I knew not what to do. After much persuasion, he induced me to take something to drink, which produced so powerful an effect upon me that I knew not what I was about; and whilst in that condition he took me to a bad house. Oh, Sir, the rest is too dreadful to relate.

He left me in the morning, and I have never seen him since. When I returned to my situation, I was discharged immediately. I went to my uncle, who would have nothing more to do with me and turned me out of his house. Having a little money left, I took a lodging and lived upon it until all was gone; and then I went on the streets to keep from starving. Two months afterward, I was taken very ill and thought I should die. A lady pitied me and obtained a letter of admission to the hospital, where I remained about a month but came out again in a bad state, and I feel I am getting worse every day. I know not where to go to obtain food and lodging; I have no money, and no one will trust me.

ANTIGONE

Antigone is a young Greek woman whose father, Oedipus, married his mother and killed his own father and left Thebes blinded and exiled. She has lived all her life in the palace of Creon, her uncle, who became king after her father's disgrace. A civil war has just ended in which both Antigone's brothers fought, one on the side of Creon and one on the opposing side. Creon has made a law that forbids anyone to perform burial rites for the bodies of the traitors. Antigone, however, has defied that law and openly performed the proscribed rites for the brother Creon named a traitor. She has been arrested and brought before Creon and asked if she has broken his law. In the following speech, Antigone's strength of conviction and her contempt for Creon is clear.

Defiance

Yes; for it was not Zeus that had published me that edict; not such are the laws set among men by the justice who dwells with the gods below; nor deemed I that thy decrees were of such force that a mortal could override the unwritten and unfailing statutes of heaven. For their life is not of today or yesterday, but from all time, and no man knows when they were first put forth.

Not through dread of any human pride could I answer to the gods for breaking *these*. Die I must—I knew that well (how should I not?)—even without thy edicts. But if I am to die before my time, I count that a gain: for when anyone lives, as I do, compassed about with evils, can such a one find aught but gain in death?

So for me to meet this doom is trifling grief; but if I had suffered my mother's son to lie in death an unburied corpse, that would have grieved me; for this, I am not grieved. And if my present deeds are foolish in thy sight, it may be that a foolish judge arraigns my folly.

Wouldst thou do more than take and slay me?

Why, then, dost thou delay? In thy discourse there is naught that pleases me—never may there be!—and so my words must need be unpleasing to thee. And yet, glory—whence could I have won a noble praise than by giving burial to mine own brother? All here would own than they thought it well, were not their lips sealed by fear. But royalty, blest in so much besides, hath the power to do and say what it will.

A VIOLENT WOMAN

The following passage is spoken by a woman who was known to co-habit with soldiers. She has a masculine appearance but good fea-tures and a good-natured expression. When asked about a rumor that she was the most violent and passionate woman in the neighborhood, she replies as follows. She's a crude and forceful speaker.

The Most Violent in the Neighborhood (1862)

Passionate! I believe you. I knocked my father down and well-nigh killed him with a flat-iron before I were twelve year old. I was a beauty then, and I ain't improved much since I've been on my own hook. I've had lots of rows with these 'ere sodgers, and they'd have slaughter'd me long before now if I had not pretty near cooked their goose. It's a good bit of it self-defense with me nowadays, I can tell you. Why, look here; look at my arm when I was run through with a bayonet once three or four years ago.

You wants to know if them rowses is common. Well, they is, and it's no good one saying they ain't, and the sodgers is such cowards they think nothing of sticking a woman once they're riled and drunk, or they'll wop us with their belts. I was hurt awful once by a blow from a belt; it hit me on the back part of the head, and I was laid up weeks in St. George's Hospital with a bad fever. The sodger who done it was jailed, but only for three months, and he swore to God as how he'd do for me the next time as he comed across me. We had words sure enough, but I split his skull with a pewter, and that shut him up for a time.

You see this bar; well, I've smashed up this place before now; I've jumped over the bar, because they wouldn't serve me without paying for it when I was hard up, and I've smashed all the tumblers and glass, and set the cocks a-going, and fought like a brick when they tried to turn me out, and it took two cops to do it; and then I lamed one of the bobbies for life by hitting him on the shin with a bit of iron—a crow or summet, I forget what it was.

How did I come to live this sort of life? Get along with your questions. If you give me more of your cheek, I'll soon serve you the same.

SOPHIA JEX-BLAKE

Sophia Jex-Blake eventually opened her own medical school, the London School of Medicine for Women, but the following speech describes the difficulty she had in attempting to gain infirmary privileges; in fact, the speech resulted in her being sued for libel by the medical student she suggested was drunk. Pioneers like Sophia Jex-Blake challenged social taboos that insisted that anatomical discussions should be limited to men. This Victorian sense of sexual privacy, however, made female patients want female doctors. The growing professionalism and prestige associated with the medical profession, however, made the resistance to women in the field even stronger. Sophia is a stout, pleasant-looking woman dressed in a suit.

Speech for Admittance to the Royal Infirmary of Edinburgh (1871)

I called on Dr. Christison, who told me curtly that the question was entirely decided in his own mind, and that it was useless for me to enter upon it. I did not call on Dr. Andrew Wood; but I was introduced to him in Sir James Simpson's room by Sir James, whose large-heartedness and large-mindedness made him from the first our warm friend and helper. On this introduction, I asked Dr. Wood to favor me with five minutes' conversation, to which his reply was that he would rather not, and turned on his heel and pursued a conversation with other persons in the room. These are specimens of the way in which a few—a very few only—met me on my arrival in Edinburgh; and I must do those few the justice to say that their conduct has been absolutely and uniformly consistent ever since. Never have we applied for educational facilities of any kind but they have done their best to meet us with an uncompromising refusal, so far as it was in their power. When the Senatus Academicus gave me leave to enter as a visitor the Botanical and Natural History classes, it was the members of this hostile clique who got a veto put on the permission. When we applied for permission merely for separate classes, exactly the same dead opposition confronted us. When, through the liberality of public feeling, this boon was granted to us, the same adversaries continued to meet us at every corner, even after one of the chiefs had stated publicly in the Senatus that, the experiment once begun, he would use every means in his power to give it a fair trial. We endeavored to make private arrangements at great expense for separate anatomical instruction; we were told repeatedly that our efforts would be useless (as indeed they proved), because certain all-powerful members of the Colleges of Physicians and Surgeons had resolved to ostracize any medical men who agreed to give us instructions. (Oh, ho.) When the absolute impossibility of getting a complete course of separate instruction drove us to ask admittance to the ordinary classes, to which several professors would willingly have admitted us, the same phalanx of opponents raised the cry of indelicacy—knowing that thus they might prevail in ranging against us public opinion, which would have been on our side had the real issue—education or no education—been declared. And now I want to point out that it was certain of these same men, who had, so to speak, pledged themselves from the first to defeat our hopes of education, and render all our efforts abortive—who, sitting in their places on the Infirmary Board, took advantage of the almost irresponsible power with which they were temporarily invested to thwart and nullify all our efforts.

JANE WELSH CARLYLE

Jane Welsh Carlyle spent most of her adult life caring for her temperamental and often bilious husband. She sacrificed her own interests and needs to make a home in which he could write—the duty and pleasure of every wife according to 19th-century standards. Jane's experience of marriage is so trying that when she hears of a young girl's intention to marry, she says, "Will you think me mad if I tell you that when I read your words 'I am going to be married,' I all but screamed? Positively, it took away my breath, as if I saw you in the act of taking a flying leap into infinite space. You had looked to me such a happy, happy little girl! your father's only daughter; and he so fond of you, as he evidently was. After you had walked out of the house together that night . . . I sat down in the dark and took 'a good cry.'" Jane is plain-spoken and practical and speaks with a Scottish accent.

The Care of a Living Author (1843)

Carlyle returned from his travels very bilious and continues very bilious up to this hour. The amount of bile that he does bring home to me, in these cases, is something "awfully grand!" Even through that deteriorating medium he could not but be struck with a "certain admiration" at the immensity of needlework I had accomplished in his absence, in the shape of chair covers, sofa covers, window curtains, and all the other manifest improvements into which I had put my whole genius and industry, and so little money as was hardly to be conceived! For three days his satisfaction over the rehabilitated house lasted; on the fourth, the young lady next door took a fit of practicing on her accursed pianoforte, which he had quite forgotten, seemingly, and he started up disenchanted in his new library, and informed heaven and earth in a peremptory manner that "there he could neither think nor live," that the carpenter must be brought back and "steps taken to make him a quiet place somewhere—perhaps best of all on the roof of the house." Then followed interminable consultations with the said carpenter, yielding, for some days, only plans (wild ones) and estimates. The roof on the house could be made all that a living author of irritable nerves could desire: silent as a tomb, lighted from above; but it would cost us 120 pounds! Impossible, seeing that we may be turned out of the house any year! So one had to reduce one's schemes to the altering of rooms that already were. By taking down a partition and instituting a fireplace where no fireplace could have been fancied capable of existing, it is expected that some bearable approximation to that ideal room in the clouds will be realized. But my astonishment and despair on finding myself after three months of what they call here "regular mess," just when I had got every trace of the work-people cleared away, and had said to myself, "Soul, take thine ease, or at all events thy swing, for thou hast carpets nailed down and furniture rubbed for many days!" just when I was beginning to lead the dreaming, reading, dawdling existence that best suits me, and alone suits me in cold weather, to find myself in the thick of a new "mess": the carpets, which I had nailed down so well with my own hands, tumbled up again, dirt, lime, whitewash, oil, paint, hard at work as before, and a prospect of new cleanings, new sewings, new arrangements stretching away into eternity for anything I see!

ANNIE BESANT

Annie Besant marries her husband because she wants to fulfill her own desire for religious work. When she loses her faith, however, she loses her husband, also. Because of her avowed atheism and advocacy for birth control, he is able to sue her as an unfit mother and win sole custody of their daughter. Later she converted to theosophy and lived the last thirty-eight years of her life in India. She is red-haired and petite and wears a tie and a beret; she is, also, a fiery and clear-minded speaker.

Decision to Marry (1866)

During that autumn I became engaged to the Reverend Frank Besant, giving up with a sigh of regret my dreams of the "religious life," and substituting for them the work that would have to be done as the wife of a priest, laboring ever in the church and among the poor. A queer view, some people may think, for a girl to take of married life, but it was the natural result of my living the life of the Early Church, of my enthusiasm for religious work. To me, a priest was a half-angelic creature, whose whole life was consecrated to heaven; all that was deepest and truest in my nature chafed against my useless days, longed for work, yearned to devote itself, as I had read women saints had done, to the service of the church and the poor, to the battling against sin and misery. "You will have more opportunity for doing good as a clergyman's wife than as anything else," was one of the pleas urged on my reluctance. My ignorance of all that marriage meant was as profound as though I had been a child of four, and my knowledge of the world was absolutely *nil*. My darling mother meant all that was happiest for me when she shielded me from all knowledge of sorrow and of sin, when she guarded me from the smallest idea of the marriage relation, keeping me ignorant as a baby till I left her home a wife. But looking back now on all, I deliberately say that no more fatal blunder can be made than to train a girl to womanhood in ignorance of all life's duties and burdens, and then to let her face them for the first time away from all the old associations, the old helps, the old refuge on the mother's breast. That "perfect innocence" may be very beautiful, but it is a perilous possession, and Eve should have the knowledge of good and of evil ere she wanders forth from the paradise of a mother's love. When a word is never spoken to a girl that is not a caress; when necessary rebuke comes in tone of tenderest reproach; when "You have grieved me" has been the heaviest penalty for a youthful fault; when no anxiety has ever been allowed to trouble the young heart—then, when the hothouse flower is transplanted, and rough winds blow upon it, it droops and fades.

LADY DOROTHY NEVILL

*The danger of the crinoline—a steel "cage" that left the legs rela-
tively unencumbered unlike the heavy petticoats—is described in this
passage by Lady Dorothy Nevill. Crinolines, which were originally
hailed as an improvement, soon were revealed to be treacherous—
they made it hard to sit down, indecent to bend over, and dangerous
to stand near fire. You must envision Lady Dorothy Nevill in the following account to be encased in a stiff yet billowing silken tent three
to five yards in circumference.*

Perils of the Crinoline (1850)

That was the day of that monstrosity "the crinoline," which once
came near to costing me my life; in fact, I only escaped a terrible fate
through mercifully retaining my presence of mind. I was in the drawing-room one evening after dinner at Dangstein before the gentlemen
had joined us, and at the time my dress caught fire I was showing a
lady an engraving of Mr. Cobden, which he had just given me and
which hung near the fireplace. Somehow or other my voluminous
dress caught fire, and in an instant I was in a blaze, but I kept my
presence of mind, and, rolling myself in the hearth rug, by some
means or other eventually beat out and subdued the flames. I was
rather badly burnt about one of my arms, where the marks remain to
this day, but otherwise I was unhurt, and, oddly enough, not at all
frightened; in fact, after having common whitening, made into a
paste with water, applied to my arm—an excellent receipt for burns
of which I had but a day or two before been reading—I came downstairs again in time to meet the gentlemen coming from their coffee.
My not having been frightened is rather puzzling, but I have an idea
that the thought of trying this new receipt took up my attention. None
of the ladies present could, of course, do much to assist me, for their
enormous crinolines rendered them almost completely impotent to
deal with fire, and had they come very close to me, all of them would
have been in a blaze, too.

A MOTHER

In the following account, a mother describes the joy and misery that motherhood entailed for women struggling to get by on too little money and without birth control. She says at the end of her account, "So here I am a woman of forty-one years, blessed with a lovely family of healthy children, faced with a big deficit, varicose veins, and an occasional loss of the use of my hands. I would like nice clothes (I've had three new dresses in fourteen years), but I must not have them yet. I'd like to develop mentally, but I must stifle that part of my nature. . . ." To shorten the selection, you could cut the paragraph that begins, "Three years later, a fifth baby came."

The Toll of Motherhood (1900)

I was married at twenty-eight in utter ignorance of the things that most vitally affect a wife and mother. My mother, a dear, pious soul, thought ignorance was innocence, and the only thing I remember her saying on the subject of childbirth was, "God never sends a babe without bread to feed it." Dame Experience long ago knocked the bottom out of that argument for me. My husband was a man earning thirty-two shillings a week—a conscientious, good man, but utterly undomesticated. A year after our marriage, the first baby was born, naturally and with little pain or trouble. I had every care, and motherhood stirred the depths of my nature. The rapture of a babe in my arms drawing nourishment from me crowned me with glory and sanctity and honor.

Alas! the doctor who attended me suffered from eczema of a very bad type in his hands. The disease attacked me, and in twenty-four hours I was covered from head to foot finally, leaving me partially and sometimes totally crippled in my hands. Fifteen months later, a second baby came—a dear little girl, and again I was in fairly good condition physically and financially, but had incurred heavy doctor's bills and attendance bills, due to my incapacity for work owing to eczema. Both the children were delicate, and dietary expenses ran high. Believing that true thrift is wise expenditure, we spent our all

trying to build up for them sound, healthy bodies, and were ill prepared financially and physically to meet the birth of a third baby sixteen months later. Motherhood ceased to be a crown of glory and became a fearsome thing to be shunned and feared.

Three years later, a fifth baby came. I was ill and tired, but my
husband fell ill a month prior to his birth, and I was up day and night.
Our doctor was, and is, one of the kindest men I have ever met. I
said: "Doctor, I cannot afford you for myself, but will you come if I
need?" "I hope you won't need me, but I'll come." I dare not let my
husband in his precarious condition hear a cry of pain from me, and
pain cannot always be stifled; and here again the doctor helped me
by giving me a sleeping draught to administer him as soon as I felt
the pains of childbirth. Hence he slept in one room while I travailed
in the other, and brought forth the loveliest boy that ever gladdened a
mother's heart.

So here I am a woman of forty-one years, blessed with a lovely
family of healthy children, faced with a big deficit, varicose veins,
and an occasional loss of the use of my hands. I would like nice
clothes (I've had three new dresses in fourteen years), but I must not
have them yet. I'd like to develop mentally, but I must stifle that part
of my nature until I have made good the ills of the past, and I am doing it slowly and surely, and my heart grows lighter, and will grow
lighter still when I know that the burden is lifted from the mothers of
our race.

SUSIE KING TAYLOR

Susie King Taylor was born a slave on one of the Sea Islands of Georgia, the eldest of six children. She was taught to read and write illegally, and during the Civil War, she became the regimental laundress, and also served as a nurse and teacher for the First South Carolina Volunteers (later known as the 33rd United States Colored Troops), the first Negro regiment. She later supported herself by teaching in the freedmen's school. She describes the difficulty of going to school "with our books wrapped in paper to prevent the police or white persons from seeing them." She went to school for two years at a freewoman's house nearby; then she had a white playmate tutor her secretly for four months; then the landlord's son, who was attending high school, tutored her. This education came in handy, as she describes below. She is tall, regal-looking, in her mid-thirties.

The Uses of Literacy (1902)

I often wrote passes for my grandmother, for all colored persons, free or slaves, were compelled to have a pass; free colored people having a guardian in place of a master. These passes were good until ten o'-clock or ten-thirty p.m. for one night or every night for one month. The pass read as follows:

Savannah, Ga., March 1, 1860.

Pass the ——— from 9:00 to 10:30 p.m.

VALENTINE GREST

Every person had to have this pass, for at nine o'clock each night a bell was rung, and any colored persons found on the street after this hour were arrested by the watchman, and put in the guardhouse until next morning, when their owners would pay their fines and release them.

About this time I had been reading so much about the "Yankees" I was very anxious to see them. The whites would tell their colored people not to go to the Yankees, for they would harness them to carts and make them pull the carts around, in place of horses.

I asked grandmother one day if this was true. She replied, "Certainly not!" that the white people did not want slaves to go over to the Yankees and told them these things to frighten them. "Don't you see those signs pasted about the streets? One reading 'I am a rattlesnake; if you touch me, I will strike!' Another reads, 'I am a wildcat! Beware,' etc. These are warnings to the North; so don't mind what the white people say."

I wanted to see these wonderful "Yankees" so much, as I heard my parents say the Yankee was going to set all the slaves free. Oh, how those people prayed for freedom! I remember, one night, my grandmother went out into the suburbs of the city to a church meeting, and they were fervently singing this old hymn—

Yes, we shall all be free,
Yes, we shall all be free,
Yes, we shall all be free,
When the Lord shall appear—

when the police came in and arrested all who were there, saying they were planning freedom, and sang "The Lord," in place of "Yankee," to blind any one who might be listening.

ANNETTE

Gothic tales were popular during the late 18th century. Such tales usually included ghosts and graveyards, evil dukes and swooning young ladies, and were read with the thrilling verve still evinced by some of Stephen King's horror stories today. In Ann Radcliffe's The Mysteries of Udolpho, *a very popular novel, the teller of the following tale is a servant girl, Annette. She's telling a fairly typical story of an unhappy maiden—crying in the castle—who disappeared one stormy night. She tells the story with obvious relish and delights in frightening herself and the young woman to whom she is recounting the story. Annette is dressed as a servant but has dangling earrings that jangle as she speaks.*

A Ghost Story (1794)

It was one evening, they say, at the latter end of the year, it might be about the middle of September, I suppose, or the beginning of October; nay, for that matter, it might be November, for that, too, is the latter end of the year, but that I cannot say for certain, because they did not tell me for certain themselves. However, it was at the latter end of the year, this grand lady walked out of the castle into the woods below, as she had often done before, all alone, only her maid was with her. The wind blew cold, and strewed the leaves trees, that we passed, ma'amselle, as we came to the castle—for Benedetto showed me the trees as he was talking—the wind blew cold, and her woman would have persuaded her to return: but all would not do, for she was fond of walking in the woods, at evening time, and, if the leaves were falling about her, so much the better.

Well, they saw her go down among the woods, but night came, and she did not return; ten o'clock, eleven o'clock, twelve o'clock came and no lady! Well, the servants thought to be sure some accident had befallen her, and they went out to seek her. They searched all night long, but could not find her, or any trace of her; and, from that day to this, ma'amselle, she has never been heard of.

They do say that the Signora has been seen several times since, walking in the woods and about the castle in the night: several of the old servants, who remained here sometime after, declare they saw her; and, since then, she has been seen by some of the vassals, who have happened to be in the castle, at night. Carlo, the old steward, could tell such things, they say, if he would.

But all this was told me for a great secret, and I am sure, ma'am, you would not hurt either me or Benedetto, so much as to go and tell it again.

E.D.E.N. SOUTHWORTH

E.D.E.N. Southworth was a prolific writer of the 19th century. Emma Dorothy Eliza Nevitte wrote eighteen novels between 1849 and 1860. She was a single mother who lived in Washington D.C. The details of her marital life (which lasted only a few years) are not known, but she was a successful writer who was able to support her two children. In the following account, she describes her experience in the terms of one of her own heroines—all the more glorious because of the depths from which she had emerged. She's a well-made-up and successful-looking woman.

Success (1854)

Let me pass over in silence the stormy and disastrous days of my wretched girlhood and womanhood—days that stamped upon my brow of youth the furrows of fifty years—let me come at once to the time when I found myself broken in spirit, health, and purse—a widow in fate but not in fact, with my babes looking up to me for a support I could not give them. It was in these darkest days of my *woman's* life that my *author's* life commenced.

The circumstances under which this, my first novel, was written, and the success that afterward attended its publication, is a remarkable instance of "sowing in tears and reaping in joy"; for, in addition to that bitterest sorrow with which I may not make you acquainted— that great life-sorrow—I had many minor troubles. My small salary was inadequate to our comfortable support. My school numbered eighty pupils, boys and girls, and I had the whole charge of them myself. Added to this, my little boy fell dangerously ill. It was too much for me. It was too much for any human being. My health broke down. I was attacked with frequent hemorrhage of the lungs. Still I persevered. I did my best by my house, my school, my sick child, and my publisher. This was indeed the very melee of the "Battle of Life." I was forced to keep up struggling when I only wished for death and for rest.

But look how it terminated. The night of storm and darkness came to an end, and morning broke on me at last—a bright, glad morning, pioneering a new and happy day of life. First of all, it was in this very tempest of trouble that my "life-sorrow" was, as it were, carried away—or I was carried away from brooding over it. Next, my child, contrary to my own opinion and the doctor's, got well. Then my book, written in so much pain, published besides in a newspaper, and, withal, being the *first* work of an obscure and penniless author, was, contrary to all probabilities, accepted by the first publishing house in America, was published and subsequently friends crowded around me—offers for contributions poured upon me. And I, who six months before had been poor, ill, forsaken, slandered, *killed* by sorrow, privation, toil, and friendlessness, found myself born as it were into a new life; found independence, sympathy, friendship, and honor, and an occupation in which I could delight. All this came very suddenly, as after a storm the sun broke.

ROXANNA

Roxanna, a businesswoman of the 18th century (a prostitute—more of a call-girl than a street-walker, though), has seduced a gentleman who thinks he has seduced her, thereby depriving her of her "virtue." He, therefore, thinks it's his duty to marry her now that she has "fallen" (a term used to describe a woman who had intercourse without being married). In the following speech, however, Roxanna argues that marriage would only compound her or any woman's trouble—not alleviate it—since once a woman married, she lost all her property and her legal identity. She is handsomely dressed, well made up, richly but not ornately bejeweled.

No Argument for Marriage (1724)

I supposed when he got to bed with me, he thought himself sure of me; and indeed, in the ordinary course of things, after he had lain with me, he ought to think so; but that, upon the same foot of argument that I had discoursed with him upon, it was just the contrary; and when a woman had been weak enough to yield up the last point before wedlock, it would be adding one weakness to another, to take the man afterward; to pin down the shame of it upon herself all the days of her life, and bind herself to live all her time with the only man that could upbraid her with it; that in yielding at first, she must be a fool, but to take the man is to be sure to be called fool; that to resist a man is to act with courage and vigor and to cast off the reproach, which, in the course of things, drops out of knowledge and dies; the man goes one way, and the woman another, as fate, and the circumstances of living direct; and if they keep one another's council, the folly is heard no more of; but to take the man is the most preposterous thing in nature, and is to befoul one's self, and live always in the smell of it. *No, no*, after a man has lain with me *as a mistress*, he ought never to lie with me *as a wife*. That's not only preserving the crime in memory, but it is recording it in the family; if the woman marries the man afterward, she bears the reproach of it to the last hour; if her husband is not a man of a hundred thousand, he sometime or other upbraids her with it; if he has children, they fail not one way or other to hear of it; if the children are virtuous, they do their mother the justice to hate her for it; if they are wicked, they give her the mortification of doing the like, and giving her for the example: On the other hand, if the man and the woman part, there is an end of the crime, and an end of the clamor; time wears out the memory of it; or a woman may remove but a few streets, and she soon outlives it, and hears no more of it.

Marriage is a dear way of purchasing ease; for very often when the trouble is taken off of our hands, so is our money, too; it is far safer for the sex not to be afraid of the trouble, but to be really afraid of our money; that if nobody is trusted, nobody will be deceived; and the staff in our own hands is the best security in the world.

LUCY

In Jane Austen's Sense and Sensibility, *Lucy confides her love and her concerns about her fiancé to her rival, pretending she doesn't know her listener is also in love with Edward. Lucy is described as sly, whith sharp eyes, and her insincerity in the following speech needs to be suggested, but not overtly. She speaks solemnly and with the deepets appearance of sincerity.*

Love's Confession

If you knew what a consolation it was to me to relieve my heart by speaking of what I am always thinking of every moment of my life, your compassion would make you overlook everything else, I am sure.

Edward only has 2000 pounds of his own. It would be madness to marry upon that; though, for my own part, I would give up every prospect of more without a sigh. I have been always used to a very small income, and could struggle with any poverty for him; but I love him too well to be the selfish means of robbing him, perhaps, of all that his mother might give him, if he married to please her. We must wait; it may be for many years. With almost every other man in the world it would be an alarming prospect, but Edward's affection and constancy nothing can deprive me of, I know.

Edward's love for me has been pretty well put to the test by our long, very long, absence, since we were first engaged, and it has stood the trial so well that I should be unpardonable to doubt it now. I can safely say that he has never gave me one moment's alarm on that account from the first.

I am rather of a jealous temper, too, by nature; and from our different situations in life, from his being so much more in the world than me, and our continual separation, I was enough inclined for suspicion to have found out the truth in an instant, if there had been the slightest alteration in his behavior to me when we met, or any lowness of spirits that I could not account for, or if he had talked more of one lady than another, or seemed in any respect less happy at

Longstaple than he used to be. I do not mean to say that I am particularly observant or quick-sighted in general, but in such a case I am sure I could not be deceived.

OLIVIA

Olivia, the actress/heroine of the 1912 novel A Woman of Genius *by Mary Austen Hunter, is torn between her sense of her own talents and ambitions on the one hand and the demands of love and domesticity on the other. She is fiercely determined to keep her own sense of the truth of her life and women's lives in general. Like many women of the period, Olivia feels smothered in the tedious, small-town drudgery of her marriage. Her husband is not financially stable, yet Olivia cannot earn any money herself. She asks, "Where is the justice in making us so that we can't do without loving and then not be happy in it?" For her, marriage means "living in one place and by a particular pattern, thinking that because you are married you have to leave off this and take up that which you wouldn't think of doing for any other reason." She concludes that "we are all wrong. People like us are after the truth of life, and marriage is the one thing that society won't take the trouble to learn the truth about." In the following monologue, Olivia, after having lost a baby and finding out that her husband's position in the Burton Brothers clothing store is precarious, has returned from her parents' house to the deadening town of Higgleston and is musing about her life. Olivia is an attractive woman in her late twenties.*

Some Sharp Truths

And if you ask me why I didn't take the chance life offers to women to justify themselves to the race, I will say that though the hope of a child presents itself sentimentally as opportunity, it figures primarily in the calculation of the majority, as a question of expense. The hard times foreseen by Burton Brothers hung black-winged in the air. We had not, in fact, been able to do more than keep up the interest on what was still due on the stock and fixtures. Nor had I even quite recovered the bodily equilibrium disturbed by my first encounter with the rending powers of life. There was a time when the spring came on in a fullness, when the procreant impulse stirred awake. I saw my-

self adequately employed shaping mean for it maybe, but the imme-
diate deterring fact was the payment to be made in August.

I went on living in Higgleston, where human intercourse was organized on the basis that whatever a woman has of intelligence and
worth over and above the sum of such capacity in man is to be ex-
cised as a superfluous growth, a monstrosity. Does anybody remember what the woman's world was like in small towns before the days
of woman's clubs? There was a world of cooking and making over;
there was a world of church-going and missionary societies and
ministerial cooperation, half grudged and half assumed as a virtue
that, since it was the only thing that lay outside themselves, was not
without extenuation. And there was another world that underlay all
this, colored and occasioned it, sicklied over with futility; it was a
world all of the care and expectancy of children overshadowed by the
recurrent monthly dread, crept about by whispers, heretical but per-
sistent, of methods of circumventing it, of a secret practice of things
openly condemned. It was a world that went half the time in faint-
hearted or unwilling or rebellious anticipation, and half on the broken
springs of what as the subject of the endless, objectionable discussions went by the name of "female complaints."

INDIANA

In the last act of The Conscious Lovers *by Richard Steele (1722), Indiana meets Mr. Sealand, who turns out to be her father, but at this point neither of them knows that. Mr. Sealand was about to agree to an engagement between his daughter, Isabella, and Mr. Bevil when he heard gossip that Bevil was involved illicitly with Indiana, whom Mr. Sealand thinks is Bevil's mistress. However, when he sees Indiana, he says, "I feared, indeed, an unwarranted passion here, but I did not think it was in abuse of so worthy an object, so accomplished a lady as your sense and mine bespeak." Indiana, as she speaks, realizes why Sealand has come. She has, up until now, hoped Bevil was in love with her. During her impassioned speech, she begins to think he has been only kind to her and that she, a friendless orphan, has mistaken his intentions. She doesn't want to spoil his chances for marriage with Isabella if that is what he wants, even at the cost of losing him. As she speaks, she becomes more and more agitated, thinking she is once more alone. If you want to shorten this speech, cut either after "What have I to do but sigh and weep, to rave, run wild, a lunatic in chains . . . my strange, strange story" or after "Why, why was I born to such a variety of sorrows?"*

The Disappointment

Tell me tenderly—keep all your suspicions concerning me alive, that you may in a proper and prepared way acquaint me why the care of your daughter obliges a person of your seeming worth and fortune to be thus inquisitive about a wretched, helpless, friendless. (*Weeping*). But I beg your pardon: though I am an orphan, your child is not; and your concern for her, it seems, has brought you hither.

But my own fears tell me all. You are the gentleman, I suppose, for whose happy daughter he is designed a husband by his good father, and he has, perhaps, consented to the overture. He was here this morning, dressed beyond his usual plainness—nay, most sumptuously—and he is to be, perhaps, this night a bridegroom.

His actions, Sir, his eyes, have only made me think he designed to make me the partner of his heart. The goodness and gentleness of his demeanor made me misinterpret all. 'Twas my own hope, my own passion, that deluded me; he never made one amorous advance to me. His large heart and bestowing hand have only helped the miserable. Nor know I why, but from his mere delight in virtue, that I have been his care, the object on which to indulge and please himself with pouring favors.

Let not me, miserable though I may be, do injury to my benefactor. No, Sir, my treatment ought rather to reconcile you to his virtues. If to bestow without a prospect of return; if to delight in supporting what might, perhaps, be thought an object of desire, with no other view than to be her guard against those who would not be so disinterested—if these actions, Sir, can in a careful parent's eye commend him to a daughter, give yours, Sir, give her to my honest, generous Bevil. What have I to do but sigh and weep, to rave, run wild, a lunatic in chains, or, hid in darkness, mutter in distracted starts and broken accents my strange, strange story?!

All my comfort must be to expostulate in madness, to relieve with frenzy my despair, and shrieking to demand of fate, "Why—why was I born to such variety of sorrows?"

'Twas heaven's high will I should be such—to be plundered in my cradle! tossed on the seas! and even there an infant captive! to lose my mother, hear but of my father! to be adopted! lose my adopter! then plunged again in worse calamities!

Yet then to find the most charming of mankind, once more to set me free from what I thought the last distress; to load me with his services, his bounties and his favors; to support my very life in a way that stole, at the same time, my very soul itself from me!

Yet then, again, this very man to take another! without leaving me the right, the pretense, of easing my fond heart with tears! For, oh! I can't reproach him, though the same hand that raised me to this height now throws me down the precipice.

BERTHA

This young prostitute's story is similar to many runaways on the streets of Los Angeles today. She ran away from home at age fifteen after her step-mother abused her. She first joined a group of men and girls haymaking, but was soon seduced by one of the men. She describes her life in London after he left her in the following passage. Bertha still has the strong arms and rosy look of a country girl, though she is decked out in cheap, loud clothing and garishly made up. You could cut after "but I never saw one that I liked" up to "I would like best to go to Australia" if you want to shorten the piece.

Life on the Streets (1862)

I came up to London in a boat from Gravesend, with other hoppers. I lived on fifteen shillings I had saved up. I lived on that as long as it lasted—more than a week. I lodged near the Dials, and used to go drinking with other women I met there, as I was fond of drink then. I don't like it so much now. We drank gin and beer. I kept to myself until my money was gone, and then I looked out for myself. I had no particular friends. The women I drank with were some bad and some good. I got acquainted with a young girl as I was walking along the Strand looking out for my living by prostitution—I couldn't starve. We walked together. We couldn't stay in the Strand, where the girls were well-dressed, and so we kept about the Dials. I didn't like it, though. Still, I thought I should never like to go home. I lodged in a backstreet near the Dials. I couldn't take anybody there. I didn't do well. I often wanted money to pay my lodgings, and food to eat, and had often to stay out all night perishing. Many a night out in the streets I never got a farthing, and had to walk about all day because I dare not go back to my room without money. I never had a fancy man. There was all sorts in the lodging-house—thirty of them— pickpockets, and beggars, and cadgers, and fancy man, and some that wanted to be fancy men, but I never saw one that I liked. I never picked pockets as other girls did; I was not nimble enough with my hands.

Sometimes I had a sovereign in my pocket, but it was never there a day. I used to go out a-drinking, treating other women, and they would treat me. We helped one another now and then. I was badly off for clothes. I had no illness except colds. The common fellows in the streets were always jeering at me. Sometimes missionaries, I think they're called, talked to me about the life I was leading, but I told them, "You mind yourself, and I'll mind myself. What is it to you where I go when I die?" I think, by the life I lead—and without help I must lead it still or starve—I sometimes get twenty shillings a week, sometimes not more than five shillings. I would like best to go to Australia, where nobody would know me. I'm sure I could behave myself there. There's no hope for me here: everybody that knows me despises me. I could take a service in Sydney. I could get rid of my swearing. I only swear now when I'm vexed—it comes out natural-like then. I could get rid of my love of drink. No one—no girl—can carry on the life I do without drink. I am strong and healthy, and could take a hard place with county work. That about Australia is the best wish I have. I'm sure sick of this life. It has only drink and excitement to recommend it.

MISS MARCHMONT

In Charlotte Brontë's novel Villette, *Miss Marchmont, an elderly maiden lady, a furrowed, gray-haired woman, grave with solitude, stern with long affliction, irritable and exacting, who has been crippled with arthritis for twenty years, is awakened one stormy night and says, "I feel young tonight, as if my affliction be about to take a turn, and I am yet destined to enjoy good health." She asks her companion to raise her up and says, "I love memory tonight . . . she is bringing back to my heart, in warm and beautiful life, realities . . . that I long have thought decayed. . . . Let me now ask . . . when my mind is so strangely clear—let me reflect why it was taken from me. For what crime was I condemned, after twelve months of bliss, to undergo thirty years of sorrow?"*

Sad Memories

One happy Christmas Eve I dressed and decorated myself, expecting my lover, very soon to be my husband, would come that night to visit me. I sat down to wait. Once more I see that moment—I see the snow-twilight stealing through the window over which the curtain was not dropped, for I designed to watch him ride up the white walk; I see and feel the soft firelight warming me, playing on my silk dress, and fitfully showing me my own young figure in a glass. I see the moon of a calm winter night, float full, clear, and cold, over the inky mass of shrubbery, and the silvered turf of my grounds. I wait, with some impatience in my pulse, but no doubt in my breast. The flames had died in the fire, but it was a bright mass yet; the moon was mounting high, but she was still visible from the lattice; the clock neared ten; he rarely tarried later than this, but once or twice he had been delayed so long.

Would he for once fail me? No—not even for once; and now he was coming—and coming fast—to atone for lost time. "Frank! you furious rider," I said inwardly, listening gladly, yet anxiously, to his approaching gallop, "you shall be rebuked for this: I will tell you it is *my* neck you are putting in peril; for whatever is yours is, in a dearer and tenderer sense, mine." There he was: I saw him; but I think tears were in my eyes, my sight was so confused. I saw the horse; I heard it stamp—I saw at least a mass; I heard a clamor. *Was* it a horse? or what heavy, dragging thing was it, crossing the strangely dark lawn? How could I name that thing in the moonlight before me? or how could I utter the feeling that rose in my soul?

I was kneeling down in the snow, beside something that lay there—something that sighed, that groaned on my breast, as I lifted and drew it to me. He was not dead; he was not quite unconscious. I had him carried in, but I gave place to none except the surgeon; and when he had done what he could, I took my dying Frank to myself. He had strength to fold me in his arms; he had power to speak my name; he heard me as I prayed over him very softly, he felt me as I tenderly and fondly comforted him.

"'Maria," he said, "I am dying in Paradise." He spent his last breath in faithful words for me. When the dawn of Christmas morning broke, my Frank was with God.

MEDEA

Fifth-century Medea is given voice in Euripides' play by that name. Although she has come to Corinth and lived as wife with Jason and borne him two children, she cannot be his legal wife by Corinthian law since she is a foreigner, and Jason has decided to leave her, marry a local princess, and take his two children with him. Medea has no legal way to stop him, and her fury frightens her neighbors, who hear her wails inside the house as she screams, "Behold what I am suffering now, though I did bind that accursed one, my husband, by strong oaths to me! O, to see him and his bride someday brought to utter destruction, they and their house with them. O, my father, my country, that I have left to my shame, after slaying my own brother." She is majestic in her rage.

Hell Hath No Fury Like a Woman Scorned

On me hath fallen this unforeseen disaster, and sapped my life; ruined I am, and long to resign the boon of existence, kind friends, and die. For he who was all the world to me, as well thou knowest, hath turned out the worst of men, my own husband. Of all things that have life and sense, we women are the most hapless creature; first must we buy a husband at a great price, and o'er ourselves a tyrant set, which is an evil worse than the first; and herein lies the most important issue, whether our choice be good or bad. For divorce is not honorable to women, nor can we disown our lords. Next must the wife, coming as she does to ways and customs new, since she hath not learnt the lesson in her home, have a diviner's eye to see how best to treat the partner of her life. If haply we perform these tasks with thoroughness and tact, and the husband live with us, without resenting the yoke, our life is a happy one; if not, 'twere best to die. But when a man is vexed with what he finds indoors, he goeth forth and rids his soul of its disgust, betaking him to some friend or comrade of like age; whilst we must need regard his single self.

And yet they say we live secure at home, while they are at the wars, with their sorry reasoning, for I would gladly take my stand in battle array three times o'er than once give birth. But enough! This language suits not thee as it does me; thou hast a city here, a father's house, some joy in life, and friends to share thy thoughts, but I am destitute, without a city, and therefore scorned by my husband, a captive I from a foreign shore, with no mother, brother, or kinsman in whom to find a new haven of refuge from this calamity. Wherefore this one boon and only this I wish to win from thee, thy silence, if haply I can some way or means devise to avenge me on my husband for this cruel treatment, and on the man who gave to him his daughter, and on her who is his wife. For though a woman be timorous enough in all else, and as regards courage, a coward at the mere sight of steel, yet in the moment she finds her honor wronged, no heart is filled with deadlier thoughts than hers.

JANE EYRE

Jane Eyre, a young woman of seventeen, trained to teach, after eight years at Lowood, a school for girls, has lost her dearest friend, Miss Temple, who has just married. She says, "My world had for some years been in Lowood: my experience had been of its rules and systems; now I remembered that the real world was wide, and that a varied field of hopes and fears, of sensations and excitement, awaited those who had the courage to go forth into its expanse, to seek real knowledge of life amidst its perils." The following speech indicates Jane's restless, seeking nature. She is poor but courageous, and her plain looks are balanced by a strength of character and a goodness of nature. If you want to shorten the following speech, you might consider cutting it either after "'grant me at least a new servitude!'" or after "if I had only a brain active enough to ferret out the means of attaining it."

A New Servitude

I went to my window, opened it, and looked out. There were the two wings of the building; there was the garden; there were the skirts of Lowood; there was the hilly horizon. My eyes passed all other objects to rest on those most remote, the blue peaks: it was those I longed to surmount; all within their boundary of rock and heath seemed prison-ground. I traced the white road winding round the base of one mountain, and vanishing in a gorge between two: how I longed to follow it further! I recalled the time when I had traveled that very road in a coach; I remembered descending that hill at twilight: an age seemed to have elapsed since the day that brought me first to Lowood, and I had never quitted it since. My vacations had all been spent at school: Mrs. Reed had never sent for me to Gateshead; neither she nor any of her family had ever been to visit me. I had no communication by letter or message with the outer world: school rules, school duties, school habits and notions, and voices, and faces, and phrases, and costumes, and preferences, and antipathies: such was what I knew of existence. And now I felt that it was not enough: I tired of the routine of eight years in one afternoon. I desired liberty; for liberty I gasped; for liberty I uttered a prayer; it seemed scattered on the wind, then faintly blowing. I abandoned it and framed a humbler supplication; for change, stimulus: that petition, too, seemed swept off into vague space: "Then," I cried, half desperate, "grant me at least a new servitude!"

A new servitude! There is something in that, I know there is, because it does not sound too sweet; it is not like such words as Liberty, Excitement, Enjoyment: delightful sounds, truly; but no more than sounds for me; and so hollow and fleeting that it is mere waste of time to listen to them. But Servitude! That must be a matter of fact. Anyone may serve: I have served here eight years; now all I want is to serve elsewhere. Can I not get so much of my own will? Is not the thing feasible? Yes—yes—the end is not so difficult; if I had only a brain active enough to ferret out the means of attaining it.

What do I want? A new place, in a new house, among new faces, under new circumstances: I want this because it is of no use wanting anything better. What do people do to get a new place? They apply to friends, I suppose: I have no friends. There are many others who have no friends, who must look about for themselves and be their own helpers; and what is their resource?

Those who want situations advertise; I must advertise—in the *Shire Herald.*

I must enclose the advertisement and the money to pay for it under a cover directed to the editor of the *Herald* I must put it, the first opportunity I have, into the post at Lowood; answers must be addressed to J.E. at the post office there. I can go and inquire in about a week after I send my letter if any are come and act accordingly.

JANE SHORE

In The Tragedy of Jane Shore, *a "she-tragedy" by Nicholas Rowe (1714), Jane's friend, Alicia, is advising her to stop grieving for the loss of King Edward VIII's love: "Still, my fair friend, still shall I find you thus? Still shall these sighs heave after one another, these trickling drops chase one another still, as if grief could overtake the hours fled far away and make old time come back?" Jane, however, protests that it's not the loss of Edward she mourns. It is her own destruction by those in power who feel she's a threat that she fears. If you would like to cut the following speech, there are two good places to stop it: either after the line "and all the pangs we feel of its decay" or after "and shelter from the storm." After the first cut, Jane gives her jewels to Alicia to hold for her in case she needs them. After the second cut, Jane extemporizes about women's fate in general.*

The Aftermath

Heaven and its saints be witness to my thoughts,
There is no hour of all my life o'erpast,
That I could wish should take its turn again.
"Tis true, the royal Edward was a wonder,
The goodly pride of all our English youth;
He was the very joy of all who saw him,
Form'd to delight, to love, and to persuade.
Impassive spirits and angelic nature
Might have been charm'd, like yielding human weakness,
Stoop'd from their heav'n and listen'd to his talking.
But what had I to do with kings and courts?
My humble lot had cast me far beneath him;
And that he was the first of all mankind,
The bravest and most lovely, was my curse.
Name him no more:
He was the bane and ruin of my peace.
This anguish and these tears, these are the legacies

His fatal love has left me. Thou wilt see me,
Believe me, my Alicia, thou wilt see me,
Ere yet a few short days pass o'er my head,
Abandon'd to the very utmost wretchedness.
The hand of pow'r has seiz'd almost the whole
Of what was left for needy life's support;
Shortly thou wilt behold me poor, and kneeling
Before thy charitable door for bread.
My form, alas! has long forgot to please;
The scene of beauty and delight is change,
No roses bloom upon my fading cheek,
But haggard grief, lean-looking, sallow care,
And pining discontent, a rueful train,
Dwell on my brow, all hideous and forlorn.
One only shadow of a hope is left me;
The noble-minded Hastings, of his goodness,
Has kindly underta'en to be my advocate,
And move my humble suit to angry Gloster.
Don't charge his generous meaning with a weakness
Which his great soul and virtue must disdain:
Too much of love thy hapless friend has prov'd,
Too many giddy, foolish hours are gone,
And in fantastic measure danc'd away:
May the remaining few know only friendship.
So thou, my dearest, truest, best Alicia,
Vouchsafe to lodge me in thy gentle heart
A partner there; I will give up mankind,
Forget the transports of increasing passion,
And all the pangs we feel its decay.
Thou art true, and only thou art true;
Therefore these jewels, once the lavish bounty
Of royal Edward's love, I trust to thee; (*Giving a casket*)
Receive this all that I can call my own,
And let it rest unknown and safe with thee:
That if the state's injustice should oppress me,
Strip me of all, and turn me out a wanderer,

My wretchedness may find relief from thee,
And shelter from the storm.
Why should I think that man will do for me
What yet he never did for wretches like me?
Mark by what partial justice we are judg'd;
Such is the fate unhappy women find,
And such the curse entail'd upon our kind,
That man, the lawless libertine, may rove
Free and unquestion'd through the wilds of love;
While woman, sense and nature's easy fool,
If poor, weak woman swerve from virtue's rule,
If, strongly charm'd, she leave the thorny way,
And in the softer paths of pleasure stray;
Ruin ensues, reproach and endless shame,
And one false step entirely damns her fame.
In vain with tears the loss she may deplore,
In vain look back to what she was before;
She sets, like stars that fall, to rise no more.

OLIVIA'S MOTHER

In Mary Hunter Austin's Woman of Genius *(1912), Olivia's mother, after two strokes, sends for Olivia, who comes to nurse her. She describes her mother: "The noble outline of her face and of her head against the pillows, the smooth hair parted Madonna-wise and brought low across her ears, the blue of her eyes looking out of the dark, swollen circles, for all her fifty-two years, with the unawakened clarity of a girl's." Her mother, feeling guilty for sending away an early lover of Olivia's and driving Olivia into what her mother suspects is an unhappy marriage, confesses in the following passage that she never really wanted Olivia's birth. She has asked Olivia (who has recently lost a baby) if she wants another child. Olivia has said it isn't yet advisable and that while she was in the hospital, the doctor told her how to prevent birth until she wants it.*

A Mother's Confession

I used to think those things weren't right, Olivia, but I don't know. Sometimes I think it isn't right, either, to bring them into the world when there is no welcome for them. You and I, Olivia, we never got on together.

But still there are things I've always wanted to tell you. When you wrote me about going on the stage, I knew there were wild things in you, Olivia, things I never looked for in a daughter of mine, things I can't understand nor account for unless—unless it was I turned you against life, my kind of life, before you were born. Many's the time I've seen you hating it and I've been harsh with you, but I wanted you should know I was being harsh with myself.

Yes, yes, I've wanted to tell you. See, it was after your father came home from the war and we were all broken up. Forester was sickly, and there was the one that died. So when I knew you were coming, I hated you, Olivia. I wanted things different. I hated you until I heard you cry. You cried all the time when you were little, Olivia, and it was I who was crying in you. I've expected some punishment would come of it.

I know they say—the scientists—that it isn't so that things before you are born can affect you as much as that.

They can say that, but we've never got on. There's things in you that aren't natural for any daughter of mine. They can say that, Olivia, but we—we know.

MILLAMANT

Congreve's The Way of the World *(1700) is a Restoration comedy that satirizes the way of the upper-class world of wit and privilege. In the following scene, Millamant, a young and pretty woman, is about to engage herself to Mirabell. As she teases him and flirts, we hear something about the customs of marriage for upper-class 18th-century couples. The speech should be played lightly, archly, flirtatiously, with all the confidence of a young woman who is secure in her lover's affection and sure of her own beauty and charm.*

Love's Demands

Vanity! No—I'll fly and be followed to the last moment. Though I am upon the very verge of matrimony, I expect you should solicit me as much as if I were wavering at the gate of a monastery, with one foot over the threshold. I'll be solicited to the very last, nay and afterward.

O, I should think I was poor and had nothing to bestow, if I were reduced to an inglorious ease, and freed from the agreeable fatigues of solicitation.

O, I hate a lover that can dare to think he draws a moment's air, independent of the bounty of his mistress. There is not so impudent a thing in nature as the saucy look of an assured man, confident of success. The pedantic arrogance of a very husband has not so pragmatical an air. Ah! I'll never marry, unless I am first made sure of my will and pleasure.

My dear liberty, shall I leave thee? My faithful solitude, my darling contemplation, must I bid you then adieu? Ay-h, adieu—my morning thoughts, agreeable wakings, indolent slumbers, all ye, adieu—I can't do it, 'tis more than impossible. Positively, Mirabell, I'll lie abed in a morning as long as I please.

And do you hear, I won't be called names after I'm married; positively I won't be called names.

Ay, as wife, spouse, my dear, joy, jewel, love, sweetheart, and the rest of that nauseous cant, in which men and their wives are so fulsomely familiar—I shall never bear that—Good Mirabell, don't let us be familiar or fond, nor kiss before folks, like my Lady Fadler and Sir Francis: nor go to Hyde Park together the first Sunday in a new chariot to provoke eyes and whispers, and then never be seen there together again; as if we were proud of one another the first week and ashamed of one another ever after. Let us never visit together, nor go to a play together, but let us be very strange and well bred: let us be as strange as if we had been married a great while; and as well bred as if we were not married at all.

I want liberty to pay and receive visits to and from whom I please; to write and receive letters, without interrogatories or wry faces on your part; to wear what I please; and choose conversation with regard only to my own taste; to have no obligation upon me to converse with wits that I don't like, because they are your acquaintance, or to be intimate with fools because they may be your relations. Come to dinner when I please, dine in my dressing room when I'm out of humor, without giving a reason. To have my closet inviolate; to be sole empress of my tea table, which you must never presume to approach without fist asking leave. And lastly, wherever I am, you shall always knock at the door before you come in. These articles subscribed, if I continue to endure you a little longer, I may by degrees dwindle into a wife.

MRS. ERLYNN

In Oscar Wilde's Lady Windermere's Fan *(1892), a drawing-room comedy with serious social undertones, we see that beneath the exterior of a socially scheming woman is the generous spirit of a mother. Mrs. Erlynn left her husband and infant daughter twenty years before. Her daughter thinks her mother's dead and worships her memory as an ideal of womanhood. At a gathering, Mrs. Erlynn discovers her daughter about to make a serious mistake and stops her. She has come to return her daughter's fan and tell her that her secret is safe; however, when she arrives, she is met by Lord Windermere, who thinks she is there to expose the truth of her parentage to his wife. He says, "For twenty years of your life you lived without your child, without a thought of your child. One day you read in the papers that she had married a rich man. You saw your hideous chance. You knew that to spare her the ignominy of learning that a woman like you was her mother, I would endure anything. You began your blackmailing." He tells her that Margaret (his wife, her daughter) kisses a "miniature of a young, innocent-looking girl with beautiful dark hair." She replies, "Ah, yes, I remember. How long ago that seems. It was done before I was married. Dark hair and an innocent expression were the fashion then." She is a very attractive woman in her forties, blonde and well-dressed, who seems to enjoy shocking and irritating the clearly disapproving Windermere. The first line is said with a note of irony, but then her voice and manner become serious. There is a note of tragedy in her tone, and, for a moment, she reveals herself. Then, after she says, "I want to live childless still," she hides her feelings with a light laugh and says, "Besides, my dear Windermere, how on earth could I pose as a mother with a grown-up daughter?" She should be dressed well and have a small hand mirror to look into—as well as, of course, Lady Windermere's fan, which she may play with as she speaks.*

A Mother

I am here to bid good-bye to my dear daughter, of course. Oh, don't imagine I am going to have a pathetic scene with her, weep on her neck and tell her who I am, and all that kind of thing. I have no ambition to play the part of a mother. Only once in my life have I known a mother's feelings. That was last night. They were terrible—they made me suffer—they made me suffer too much. For twenty years, as you say, I have lived childless—I want to live childless still. Besides, my dear Windermere, how on earth could I pose as a mother with a grown-up daughter? Margaret is twenty-one, and I have never admitted that I am more than twenty-nine, or thirty at the most. Twenty-nine where there are pink shades, thirty when there are not. So you see what difficulties it would involve. No, as far as I am concerned, let your wife cherish the memory of this dead, stainless mother. Why should I interfere with her illusions? I find it hard enough to keep my own. I lost one illusion last night. I thought I had no heart. I find I have, and a heart doesn't suit me, Windermere. Somehow it doesn't go with modern dress. It makes one look old. (*She takes up a hand-mirror from table and looks into it.*) And it spoils one's career at critical moments.

I suppose, Windermere, you would like me to retire into a convent, or become a hospital nurse, or something of that kind, as people do in silly modern novels. That is stupid of you, Arthur; in real life we don't do such things—not so long as we have any good looks left, at any rate. No, what consoles one nowadays is not repentance, but pleasure. Repentance is quite out of date. And besides, if a woman really repents, she has to go to a bad dressmaker, otherwise no one believes in her. And nothing in the world would induce me to do that. No; I am going to pass entirely out of your two lives. My coming into them has been a mistake—I discovered that last night.

If you tell her who I am, I will make my name so infamous that it will mar every moment of her life. I will ruin her and make her wretched. If you dare to tell her, there is no depth of degradation I will not sink to, no pit of shame I will not enter. You shall not tell her—I forbid you.

NORA

Ibsen's A Doll's House *shocked 19th-century London audiences. When Nora, the heroine, leaves her husband and children to find out for herself what life is, the audience left also. In the play, at the beginning, Nora is a happy wife and mother, a "songbird" as her husband, Torvald, calls her. In the course of the play, we discover Nora borrowed money years before to save Torvald's life, but since women couldn't legally borrow money and since her father was ill also, Nora forged his signature. She has been paying off the loan secretly over the years. When Torvald finds out what she did, he says she ruined him and that she is not a fit mother for their children. When, however, he finds out it will not be exposed, he "forgives" Nora, saying, "You must not think anymore about the hard things I said in my first moment of consternation, when I thought everything was going to overwhelm me. I have forgiven you, Nora." But Nora has seen how easily she could lose what he says is his love for her—how he could turn on her so completely, and says, "You don't understand me, and I have never understood you either—before tonight." In his story of the superficiality of a middle-class marriage, Ibsen exposed the emptiness behind the drawing-room curtains of many lives. In the following speech, Nora tells her husband what she has learned about their marriage. She is a pretty woman in her late twenties, dressed to leave the house.*

The Doll Wife

That is just it; you have never understood me. I have been greatly wronged, Torvald—first by papa and then by you.

You have never loved me. You have only thought it pleasant to be in love with me.

It is perfectly true, Torvald. When I was at home with papa, he told me his opinion about everything, and so I had the same opinions; and if I differed from him, I concealed the fact because he would not have liked it. He called me his doll-child, and he played with me just as I used to play with my dolls. And when I came to live with you—

I mean that I was simply transferred from papa's hands into yours. You arranged everything according to your own taste, and so I got the same tastes as you—or else I pretended to, I am really not quite sure which—I think sometimes the one and sometimes the other. When I look back on it, it seems to me as if I had been living here like a poor woman—just from hand to mouth. I have existed merely to perform tricks for you, Torvald. But you would have it so. You and papa have committed a great sin against me. It is your fault that I have made nothing of my life.

I have been merry, but never happy. And you have always been so kind to me. But our home has been nothing but a playroom. I have been your doll-wife, just as at home I was papa's doll-child; and here the children have been my dolls. I thought it great fun when you played with me, just as they thought it great fun when I played with them. That is what our marriage has been, Torvald.

I no longer believe that I am a wife and a mother.

I believe that before all else I am a reasonable human being, just as you are—or, at all events, that I must try and become one. I know quite well, Torvald, that most people would think you right, and that views of that kind are to be found in books; but I can no longer content myself with what most people say, or with what is found in books. I must think over things for myself and get to understand them.

MISS JULIE

In Miss Julie *by August Strindberg (1888), he says "Miss Julie is a modern character, not that the half-woman, the man-hater, has not always existed, but because now that she has been discovered, she has stepped to the front and begun to make a noise." He goes on to say, "Degenerate men seem instinctively to choose their mates from among such women. . . . But fortunately they perish because they cannot come to terms with reality. . . . The type is tragic." In the play, there are only two main characters, Miss Julie (aged twenty-five) and her valet, Jean, and one minor character, a cook named Kristin. The action centers on the seduction of Miss Julie by Jean and her ensuing breakdown. After the confession she makes below, Jean taunts her and finally encourages her to commit suicide. In the following scene, she drinks as she talks and seems to take pleasure in showing Jean that he didn't seduce a "lady" as he thought he did.*

My Past

Listen. My mother wasn't well-born; she came of quite humble people and was brought up with all those new ideas of sex-equality and women's rights and so on. She thought marriage was quite wrong. So when my father proposed to her, she said she would never become his *wife*, but in the end she did. I came into the world, as far as I can make out, against my mother's will, and I was left to run wild, but I had to do all the things a boy does—to prove women are as good as men. I had to wear boys' clothes; I was taught to handle horses—and I wasn't allowed in the dairy. She made me groom and harness and go out hunting; I even had to try to plough. All the men on the estate were given the women's jobs, and the women the men's, until the whole place went to rack and ruin and we were the laughing-stock of the neighborhood. At last my father seems to have come to his senses and rebelled. He changed everything and ran the place his own way. My mother got ill—I don't know what was the matter with her, but she used to have strange attacks and hide herself in the attic or the garden. Sometimes she stayed out all night. Then came the great fire that you have heard people talking about. The house and the stables and the barns—the whole place burnt to the ground. In very suspicious circumstances. Because the accident happened the very day the insurance had to be renewed, and my father had bought the new premium, but through some carelessness of the messenger it arrived too late. (*She refills her glass and drinks.*)

We were destitute and had to sleep in the carriages. My father didn't know how to get money to rebuild, and then my mother suggested he should borrow from old friend of hers, a local brick manufacturer. My father got the loan and, to his surprise, without having to pay interest. So the place was rebuilt.

(*Drinks.*) Do you know who set fire to it? My mother.

Do you know who the brick manufacturer was? My mother's lover.

Do you know whose the money was? It was my mother's.

There wasn't any settlement. My mother had a little money of her own, which she didn't want my father to control, so she invested it with her friend. Who grabbed it.

He appropriated it. My father came to know all this. He couldn't bring an action, couldn't pay his wife's lover, nor prove it was his wife's money. That was my mother's revenge because he made himself master in his own house. He nearly shot himself then—at least there's a rumor he tried and didn't bring it off. So he went on living, and my mother had to pay dearly for what she'd done. Imagine what those five years were like for me. My natural sympathies were with my father, yet I took my mother's side, because I didn't know the facts. I'd learnt from her to hate and distrust men—you know how she loathed the whole male sex. And I swore to her I'd never become the slave of any man.

LYSISTRATA

*Lysistrata by Aristophanes (411 B.C.) is a ribald comedy that explic-
itly links war and sex in a unique way—the women of Athens and
Sparta, tired of the Peloponnesian War (which lasted twenty-nine
years), deny their husbands and lovers sex until they agree to stop
the war. In a brilliantly strategic move, Lysistrata (whose name
means "she who disbands the army") also has the women take
refuge in the Acropolis, where the money is kept so that the men also
have no money to wage war. In the following speech, Lysistrata is
explaining the women's plan to end the war to a horrified old magis-
trate.*

War, Woman-Style

Formerly we endured the war for a good long time with our usual
restraint, no matter what you men did. You wouldn't let us say
"boo," although nothing you did suited us. But we watched you well,
and though we stayed at home, we'd often hear of some terribly
stupid measure you'd proposed. Then, though grieving at heart, we'd
smile sweetly and say, "What was passed in the Assembly today
about writing on the treaty-stone?"

"What's that to you?" my husband would say. "Hold your
tongue!" And I held my tongue.

So I kept still at home. Then we'd hear of some plan still worse
than the first; we'd say, "Husband, how could you pass such a stupid
proposal?" He'd scowl at me and say, "If you don't mind your
spinning, your head will be sore for weeks. *War shall be the concern
of Men.*"

Now there's not a *man* left in the country. No, not one. Therefore,
all we women have decided in council to make a common effort to
save Greece.

How long should we have waited? Now, if you're willing to listen
to our excellent proposals and keep silence for us in your turn, we
still may save you.

If only sweet Eros and the Cyprian Queen of Love shed charm over our breasts and limbs and inspire our men with amorous longing and priapic spasms, I think we may soon be called Peacemakers among the Greeks.

Just like a ball of wool, when it's confused and snarled: we take it thus, and draw out a thread here and a thread there with out spindles; thus we'll unsnarl this war, if no one prevents us, and draw together the various states with embassies here and embassies there.

First you ought to treat the city as we do when we wash the dirt out of a fleece: stretch it out and pluck and thrash out of the city all those prickly scoundrels; aye, and card out those who conspire and stick together to gain office, pulling off their heads. Then card the wool, all of it, into one fair basket of goodwill, mingling in the aliens residing here, any loyal foreigners, and anyone who's in debt to the Treasury; and consider that all our colonies lie scattered 'round about like remnants; from all of these collect the wool and gather it together here, wind up a great ball, and then weave a good stout cloak for the democracy.

LADY BOOBY

Henry Fielding's tale of a handsome footman, Joseph Andrews, in
The Adventures of Joseph Andrews, *is a typically raucous and las-
civious novel recounting the many attempts made on Joseph's virtue
by all the women of any class who see him. Fielding takes satirical
aim at all the 18th-century novels that dramatize the trials of young,
virtuous maidens by simply placing his young hero in similar situations. In fact, Joseph Andrews is the brother of the heroine of a very
popular sentimental novel of the day,* Pamela: or Virtue Rewarded.
*In her novel, Pamela virtuously evades all her young master's at-
tempts to seduce her and ends up marrying him and becoming Lady
Pamela. For poor Joseph, however, Lady Booby, his mistress, has
less honorable intentions. In the following soliloquy, Lady Booby
tries to reason herself out of her passion for the handsome young
footman. Her oscillation should be clear throughout and her lust for
Joseph should be manifest. She should be a little blowzy, a little over
made up, clearly middle-aged but not totally unattractive.*

Help Me Help Myself

What am I doing? How do I suffer this passion to creep impercepti-
bly upon me? How many days are passed since I could have submit-
ted to ask myself the question? Marry a footman! Distraction! Can I
afterward bear the eyes of my acquaintance? But I can retire from
them; retire with one in whom I propose more happiness than the
world without him can give me! Retire—to feed continually on
beauties that my inflamed imagination sickens with eagerly gazing
on; to satisfy every appetite, every desire, with their utmost wish.
Ha! and do I dote thus on a footman! I despise, I detest my passion.
Yet why? Is he not generous, gentle, kind?

—Kind to whom? To the meanest wretch, a creature below my
consideration. Doth he not?

—Yes, he doth prefer her; curse his beauties, and the little low
heart that possesses them; which can basely descend to this despicable wench, and be ungratefully deaf to all the honors I do him.

—And can I love this monster? No, I will tear his image from my bosom, tread on him, spurn him. I will have those pitiful charms, which now I despise, mangled in my sight; for I will not suffer the little jade I hate to riot in the beauties I condemn. No, though I despise him myself; though I would spurn him from my feet, was he to languish at them, no other should taste the happiness I scorn. Why do I say happiness? To me it would be misery.

—To sacrifice my reputation, my character, my rank in life, to the indulgence of a mean and a vile appetite.

—How I detest the thought! How much more exquisite is the pleasure resulting from the reflection of virtue and prudence than the faint relish of what flows from vice and folly! Whither did I suffer this improper, this mad passion to hurry me, only by neglecting to summon the aids of reason to my assistance? Reason, which hath now set before me my desires in their proper colors, and immediately helped me to expel them. Yes, I thank heaven and my pride, I have now perfectly conquered this unworthy passion; and if there was no obstacle in its way, my pride would disdain any pleasures that could be the consequence of so base, so mean, so vulgar a passion.

ORDER DIRECT

MONOLOGUES THEY HAVEN'T HEARD, Karshner. Modern speeches written in the language of today. $8.95.

MORE MONOLOGUES THEY HAVEN'T HEARD, Karshner. More exciting living-language speeches. $8.95.

SCENES THEY HAVEN'T SEEN, Karshner. Modern scenes for men and women. $7.95.

FOR WOMEN: MONOLOGUES THEY HAVEN'T HEARD, Pomerance. Contemporary speeches for actresses. $8.95

MONOLOGUES FOR KIDS, Roddy. 28 wonderful speeches for boys and girls. $8.95.

MORE MONOLOGUES for KIDS, Roddy. More great speeches for boys and girls. $8.95.

SCENES for KIDS, Roddy. 30 scenes for girls and boys. $8.95.

MONOLOGUES for TEENAGERS, Karshner. Contemporary teen speeches. $8.95.

SCENES for TEENAGERS, Karshner. Scenes for today's teen boys and girls. $7.95.

HIGH-SCHOOL MONOLOGUES THEY HAVEN'T HEARD, Karshner. Contemporary speeches for high-schoolers, $7.95.

DOWN-HOME, Karshner. Great character speeches for men and women in the language of rural America. $7.95.

MONOLOGUES from the CLASSICS, ed. Karshner. Speeches from Shakespeare, Marlowe, and others. An excellent collection for men and women, $7.95.

SCENES from the CLASSICS, ed. Maag. Scenes from Shakespeare and others. $7.95.

SHAKESPEARE'S MONOLOGUES THEY HAVEN'T HEARD, ed. Dotterer. Lesser-known speeches from The Bard. $7.95.

MONOLOGUES from CHEKHOV, trans. Cartwright. Modern translations from Chekhov's major plays: *Cherry Orchard, Uncle Vanya, Three Sisters, The Sea gull.* $8.95.

MONOLOGUES from GEORGE BERNARD SHAW, ed. Michaels. Great speeches for men and women from the works of G.B.S. $7.95.

MONOLOGUES from OSCAR WILDE, ed. Michaels. The best of Wilde's urbane, dramatic writing from his greatest plays. For men and women. $7.95.

WOMAN, Pomerance. Monologues for actresses. $8.95.

MODERN SCENES for WOMEN, Pomerance. Scenes for today's actresses. $7.95.

MONOLOGUES from MOLIÈRE, trans. Dotterer. A definitive collection of speeches from the French Master. The first translation into English prose. $9.95.

SHAKESPEARE'S MONOLOGUES for WOMEN, ed. Dotterer. $8.95.

DIALECT MONOLOGUES, Karshner/Stern. 13 essential dialects applied to contemporary monologues. Book and cassette tape. $19.95.

YOU SAID a MOUTHFUL, Karshner. Tongue twisters galore. Great exercises for actors, singers, public speakers. Fun for everyone. $7.95.

TEENAGE MOUTH, Karshner. Modern monologues for young men and women. $8.95.

SHAKESPEARE'S LADIES, ed. Dtterer. A second book of Shakespeare's monologues for women. With a descriptive text on acting Shakespeare. $7.95.

BETH HENLEY: MONOLOGUES FOR WOMEN, Henley. *Crimes of the Heart*, others. $7.95.

CITY WOMEN, Smith. 20 powerful, urban monologues. Great audition pieces. $7.95.

KIDS' STUFF, Roddy. 30 great audition pieces for children. $7.95.

KNAVES, KNIGHTS, AND KINGS, ed. Dotterer. Shakespeare's speeches for men. $8.95.

DIALECT MONOLOGUES, VOL. II, Karshner/Stern. 14 more important dialects. Farsi, Afrikaans, Asian Indian, etc. Book and cassette tape. $19.95.

RED LICORICE, Tippit. 31 great scene-monologues for preteens. $8.95.

MODERN MONOLOGUES FOR MODERN KIDS, Mauro. $7.95.

A WOMAN SPEAKS: WOMEN FAMOUS, INFAMOUS and UNKNOWN, ed. Cosentino. $12.95.

FITTING IN, Mauro. Modern monoloues for boys and girls. $8.95.

VOICES, ed. Cosentino. Scene-study pieces for women. $12.95.

FOR WOMEN: MORE MONOLOGUES THEY HAVEN'T HEARD, Pomerance. $8.95

Send your check or money order (no cash or COD) plus handling charges of $4.00 for the first book and $1.50 for each additional book. California residents add 8.25 % tax. Send your order to: Dramaline Publications, 36-851 Palm View Road, Rancho Mirage, California 92270.